THE COMPLETE

A comprehens
and using

THE COMPLETE SPROUTING BOOK

A Guide to Growing and Using Sprouted Seeds

by

Per and Gita Sellmann

Translated from the Swedish by Kit Zweigbergk and Palden Jenkins

THORSONS PUBLISHERS LIMITED
Wellingborough, Northamptonshire

First published in Sweden as *Allt om Groddar*
First English edition 1981
First published in this series 1984
Second Impression 1986

© THORSONS PUBLISHERS LIMITED 1984

This book is sold subject to the condition that it shall not, by way of trade or otherwise, be lent, re-sold, hired out, or otherwise circulated without the publisher's prior consent in any form of binding or cover other than that in which it is published and without a similar condition including this condition being imposed on the subsequent purchaser.

British Library Cataloguing in Publication Data

Sellmann, Per
   The complete sprouting book.
   1. Cookery (sprouts)
   I. Title   II. Sellmann, Gita
   III. Allt om Groddar. *English*
   641.6   TX801

ISBN 0-7225-0966-9

Printed and bound in Great Britain

Contents

	Page
Introduction	7

Chapter
1. The Nutritional Value of Sprouts — 13
2. Sprouts and Grasses – A Healing Diet — 19
3. Sprouts in Children's Food — 25
4. The Ecological Advantages of Sprouts — 27
5. Check List for Beginners — 29
6. Sprouting in Your Own Kitchen — 35
7. Sprouting Methods — 39
8. Sprouting While Travelling — 51
9. Sprout Directory — 55
10. Wheatgrass and Sunflower Cultivation Indoors — 67
11. Practical Cooking Hints — 73
12. Sprout Recipes — 77

Further Information — 123
Bibliography — 125
Index — 127

Introduction

CHEAP, HEALTHY AND TASTY
It is remarkable that while the great value of sprouts as food for humans has been known in the East for thousands of years, westerners have only recently come to appreciate them. During his voyages in the South Seas in the eighteenth century, Captain Cook made a courageous and welcome experiment with them, but this made no lasting impression on our daily fare. In our part of the world, the only propagators of sprouts have for a long time been Chinese restaurants until after World War II when Ann Wigmore, director of a famous Health Institute in Boston, started her pioneer work to spread the use of sprouts as a basic nutritional source to wider circles.

NATURAL LIFE ENERGY
Nowadays we flounder around in a sea of different refined and chemicalized variations of convenience food, and are swamped with seductive advertising which gives fancy promises of fantastic new taste sensations; and then, all of a sudden, we fall upon a few simple little bean

sprouts setting up in competition with the more sophisticated and complex foodstuffs. Usually we soak beans as a prelude to cooking them, but now we can do it to let them expand, sprout and push out dainty little leaves and roots. The enormous life potential in nature is revealed before our very eyes in a few simple glass bottles which do not even contain any soil. It's almost like magic. A handful of alfalfa seeds grow sevenfold in just a few days. And the magic spell has comprised only water, warmth and a touch of loving care. Nowadays you don't often get so much for so little.

CHANGES IN ESTABLISHED CULINARY HABITS

Food traditions, like so many other cultural manifestations, have changed with time, sometimes for the better and sometimes for the worse. People have always sought to improve their standard of living, but in their zeal they have made some fatal mistakes. Our natural and nutritious foods have for too long been debilitated and transmogrified, subjected to all sorts of synthetic colourings, stabilizers and emulsifiers, and now we are paying the price with new diseases and allergies. All these additives give our food a false semblance of freshness, presentability and quality when all these factors are actually often lacking. Only now do we realize that even minute doses of chemicals added to food and drink can be directly harmful to people, animals and nature. At last, voices of protest are making themselves heard in a growing number all over the world.

LIVE MORE CHEAPLY AND SAVE ENERGY

Interest in natural and untreated foods is growing in tempo with this increasing protest against harmful additives and expensive food processing. The imported fruit and vegetables we find in the shops during the winter months are not only expensive but also highly treated to enable them to keep during transportation and storage. That is why our home-grown sprouts are so invaluable in the winter season.

Of course, we do not mean that one ought to live on

Sprouted seeds: a meal in themselves

sprouts alone. But if we use sprouts as a major part of our diet in certain seasons we can drastically cut food costs, and begin to calculate our food budget again in pennies instead of pounds. Even if we only use sprouts as a supplement to ordinary home cooking or wholefoods, we can save a lot. Since we ourselves buy and grow the seeds, we cut out the middleman and all the costly packaging, marketing and transport involved in more commonly used foods. Not only this, but eating sprouts fresh or just lightly cooked, we save energy by not using the oven.

AN ALL-ROUND AND WHOLESOME FOOD

Nowadays it is difficult to believe that something can be both inexpensive and good. So let's have a look at the nutritional value of sprouts.

Since they are a relatively new phenomenon in the West, there is little detailed information on their nutritional elements; yet research has been intensifying everywhere, especially in the USA and India, and even in Japan and Israel. In Sweden the State Food Administration has particularly examined mung and chickpea sprouts.

There are still many unanswered questions, but it is already clear that sprouts belong to the group of so-called all-round foodstuffs; that is, those containing a wide range of nutritional elements. Researchers have noted, amongst other things, the fantastic multiplication of vitamins, especially vitamin C, during the sprouting process.

Research papers also verify the presence of both high-quality proteins and many of the trace elements vital for humans. On the other hand the experts are still arguing about the pros and cons of eating sprouts raw or slightly cooked. One of the main arguments for light cooking is that the protein in sprouts becomes thereby more digestible.

But we need patience in waiting for research results. Nutrition is a very young field, and many of yesterday's truths no longer hold. Not long ago most nutrition

From seeds to sprouts

researchers were united in advising against a wholly vegetarian way of life. Now there is suddenly a much more positive attitude, and vegetarian foods are seen as a worthy alternative to the ordinary everyday diet. There are sure to be many rounds in the nutritional debate before ideas about the vital sprouts are straightened out.

TASTY VARIETY IN YOUR MENU

Healthy and inexpensive. So far, so good. But what about taste? For centuries it has almost totally dominated our choice of food. All kinds of gastronomical tricks have been exalted, even up to the level of winning culinary medals, regardless of whether they have been health-giving or not. Eating good food together with others has become an important social event, and the things we stuff inside ourselves form a regular theme in conversation.

Many people are curious about new foods, while others are very conservative in their habits, being suspicious about anything new. Many have doubts about these 'strange' sprouts. Dare one eat them? What do they taste like? But most people, both young and old, think sprouts taste really good. And everyone seems to have a particular favourite.

But even sprouts demand a certain culinary care so that they titillate the taste buds in the best way. It depends on *how* you grow, prepare and combine them in different dishes. And that's also what this book deals with. Because enjoying our meals, and even making them a feast for the eyes, is what the whole exercise is all about.

1
The Nutritional Value of Sprouts

It may be hard to believe, but the insignificant little sprout in fact contains more concentrated and more digestible nutrition than the dry seed or the mature plant. In the sprout all the potential substances are released that one day will be used to develop it into a fully grown plant.

The low metabolism of the dormant dry seed is drastically changed just by placing it in water. Many intricate chemical processes start at once. All these changes are mainly due to the greatly increased enzyme activity which occurs during the sprouting period.

The caloric value is reduced by 10-20 per cent and the carbohydrates are changed into sugars. Saturated fats become mainly polyunsaturated and proteins are broken down into their component amino acids. The flatulence problems of beans are also greatly reduced through sprouting, the enzyme activity making sprouts easier to digest than dry seeds and beans.

Perhaps the most remarkable changes are the synthesis of different vitamins, e.g. vitamin E and the B-complex, but especially vitamin C. Being hardly measurable in the

Fresh tender sprouts, packed with goodness and grown in the kitchen

dry beans, some bean sprouts show an increase of several hundred per cent in vitamin C. This was discovered 200 years ago but was then neglected.

After about eight days of sprouting the vitamin content of the sprouts begins to reduce again. It is also interesting to note that seeds growing in lower temperatures do not only grow more slowly, but also form more vitamin C than those growing under warmer conditions.

Some of the minerals and other substances leach out in the water used during the sprouting process, but the remaining minerals change into a form that can be directly assimilated by the human body. The chlorophyll formed when sprouts are exposed to light is another valuable asset, as is carotene, which is also greatly increased.

All the above-mentioned changes clearly indicate that sprouts are much more easily digested and also more rich in nutrition than the original dry seeds and beans. There are still a number of contradictory findings and many unanswered questions amongst researchers concerning certain aspects of the sprouting process. But it is clear that the changes that occur as seeds turn to sprouts are highly beneficial to humans.

In literature about sprouts one often comes across very different interpretations and figures as to the nutritional content and its increment in seeds, beans and sprouts. To really appreciate such figures and tables one has however to be quite familiar with nutritional terms and the various systems of measurement used by the experts. Furthermore, to compare different tables it is also necessary to understand under what conditions the experiments have been carried out, e.g. what day in the sprouting process the readings were taken, in what temperature and lighting the sprouting was done, etc. let us therefore just give you two examples of such tables to show the trend.

The first one is from an American researcher, Paul Burkholder, and his study of oats at Yale University. After five days sprouting he obtained the following increases of vitamin B2-complex in comparison to the dry seed.

	%
Nicotinic acid	500
Biotin	50
Pantothenic acid	200
Pyridoxine (B6)	500
Folic acid	600
Inositol	100
Thiamin (B1)	10
Riboflavin (B2)	1350

Dr C.W. Bailey of the University of Minnesota has obtained a similar large increase in the whole vitamin B complex, as well as an increase of 600 per cent in vitamin C from sprouted oats.

The table opposite is taken from the *American Journal of Food Science*, Volume 40, 1975.

The Swedish National Food Administration is also carrying out research into the value of sprouts as food for human beings especially the vitamin and mineral value of chick peas and mung beans. The Institute has a lively correspondence with researchers and institutions in India, the USA and other countries where a considerable amount of study on sprouts has already been carried out. These studies, however, are only a drop in the ocean compared to what needs to be done in this area. More and more nutritionalists seem convinced that sprouts are vitally important as food source for man and that much more research will be devoted to sprouts in the future.

Nutrients per 100 calories

	Wt. (g)	Protein (g)	Fat (g)	Fiber (g)	Thiamine (mg)	Riboflavin (mg)	Niacin (mg)	Vitamin C (mg)	Calcium (mg)	Iron (mg)	Zinc (mg)
ALFALFA											
seeds	26	9.0	3.2	2.0	0.28	0.15	0.5	7	43	3.3	1.8
sprouts	244	12.4	1.5	4.1	0.34	0.51	3.9	39	68	3.4	2.4
LENTILS											
seeds	29	7.7	0.5	1.4	0.21	0.09	0.9	2	10	3.8	1.4
sprouts	96	8.1	0.3	1.1	0.20	0.09	1.1	23	12	2.9	3.0
MUNG BEANS											
seeds	30	6.9	0.4	1.5	0.21	0.14	0.5	—	25	3.5	1.1
sprouts	189	8.1	0.4	1.1	0.26	0.34	2.1	38	25	3.6	1.7
SOYBEANS											
seeds	23	8.9	4.7	1.2	0.28	0.05	0.7	—	51	0.35	1.4
sprouts	95	11.4	2.5	2.2	0.30	0.15	1.1	11	77	0.4	1.5
RDA*		46	**	**	1.0	1.2	13	45	800	18	15

*RAD Recommended Daily Dietary Allowances for women 23-50 years old, 5'5", weighing 128 pounds.
**RDA not established
Modified from *Journal of Food Science*, Volume 40 (1975)
g = grams (28 grams = 1 ounce)
mg = milligrams

Sprouts — a big return for a small outlay

2
Sprouts and Grasses — A Healing Diet

Going back into the past, sprouts have at different times been used as both food and medicine, and this is probably where the secret lies. As far back as 400 B.C. the Greek physician Hippocrates said, 'Let your food be your medicine'.

Apart from their historical role as a remedy for scurvy and certain animal diseases, sprouts have not yet aroused the interest they really merit among modern scientists. Very little scientific research has as yet been done on their alleged effect on illnesses of different kinds.

If an unsuitable food can make you ill, a better diet can certainly make you healthy, and for better health sprouts and grasses certainly have an important role to play. Their high nutritional value is being appreciated by more and more people all over the world.

At a medical gathering in New York in 1977, John H. Knowles from the Research Centre of the Rockefeller Foundation emphasized that the greatest advances in health care will probably not come from the test tube or the clinic but from individual self-care in the form of wiser living.

Ann Wigmore, the foremost American pioneer in advocating sprouts as human food sources, also stressed the importance of including grass and grass juice with your daily food. She is often thought of as a crazy herbalist whose extreme grass and sprout diets are literally too hard for most people to swallow. For the culinary gourmet giving highest priority to taste, simple grass eating sounds downright degrading. Animal fodder! Exactly, and that's precisely where the clue lies. Many animals, even of considerable size, keep in excellent health from birth to death mainly by eating simple grass. The American scientist Dr Earp-Thomas, who researched into soil utilization and grasses, expressed in a letter to Ann Wigmore his great surprise that more attention had not been given to grass as food for human beings.

Some doctors maintain that the chlorophyll of wheatgrass cleans and builds up resistance in the bodily system, while at the same time neutralizing toxic poisons. At Temple University in Philadelphia, chlorophyll has been used with good results against ear, nose and throat maladies. Dr Hans Fischer, the German Nobel Prize winner, even used chlorophyll against anaemia.

Do sprouts and common grass then really have genuine healing properties? The greater majority of orthodox medical doctors say 'no'; the more holistically oriented New Age doctors say 'Yes', and the testimonies of people who have been cured by using a sprout and grass based diet are innumerable.

Ann Wigmore, director of the famous Hippocrates Health Institute in Boston, is herself a glowing testimony to what such a diet can do. And yet, it's very hard to believe that this vital 'old lady' was on so many occasions close to giving up. Referring to the results at her institute, she maintains that she has still not seen one single case that has not benefited greatly from a 'diet treatment' of sprouts and wheatgrass. Then of course the health of the patient depends very much on whether he will change his former eating habits and fulfil the new regime when coming home again.

SPROUTS AND GRASSES – A HEALING DIET

Ann Wigmore was born in Lithuania and grew up on a homestead surrounded by fields and forests. When her parents emigrated to the United States she was a very weak and sickly child and had to remain with her grandmother. This old lady, who was a herbal doctor, was able to cure Ann by using natural remedies including mudbaths and herbal medicines. Her grandmother also gave Ann the background knowledge of the healing properties of sprouts and grasses for which, later in life, she would discover such a wide audience.

At the age of sixteen, Ann also finally moved to the United States and in her wish for quick assimilation into her new homeland she very soon adopted the lifestyle offered by the expanding modern industrialized American society. She was easily seduced by all the attractive plastic packages and appealingly labelled tins on the shop shelves. By the time Ann was approaching fifty the 'high' standard of American life had changed her into a physical wreck. Sundry infections and one illness after another had left her very weak. Rheumatism in her joints had become so bad that she could hardly walk, but no orthodox medical approach seemed able to help her.

It was then that she recalled her grandmother's teachings, and she began experimenting with different herbs and even common weeds. Many thought her mad as she went gathering bunches of herbs along ditches and hedgerows and picking weeds in the Boston parks. But Ann did not give up.

Wheatgrass juice and sprouts with additions of raw vegetables and fresh fruit became Ann's diet during the following years and slowly but surely her health and happiness returned. During these years of seeking out a new lifestyle she met many like-minded people and this convinced her that she was on the right track. Soon she also received further encouragement for her theories from researchers both within the USA and abroad.

In 1963 Ann Wigmore was finally able to open her Health Institute. It was named the Hipprocrates Health Institute after the Greek founder of medicine and is located in an old mansion in the centre of Boston. From there she started her work of spreading information about the high nutritional value of sprouts and wheatgrass through books, courses, television demonstrations and lectures all over the world. Raw, unboiled, uncooked sprouts and grasses, together with vegetables and fruits, became the basic food at this institute, which also became famous for its ovenless kitchen.

Some of the people that were cured by Ann's diet also became her assistants and collaborators at the institute. One of them, Viktoras Kulvinskas, left a promising scientific career to follow in Ann's footsteps. He has written several health books advocating sprouts and grasses and also lectures about a new way of life all over the USA. Another of her collaborators, Stan Kalson, a qualified polarity therapist, who cured both his overweight and his ear and nose problems with her diet, is now the director of his own Holistic Health Center. Several other health institutes both in the USA and in Europe have adopted Ann Wigmore's ideas to a lesser or greater extent.

The best known case of cure, however, is that of Mrs Eydie Mae Hunsberger, who wrote the book *How I Conquered Cancer Naturally*. She describes how she developed breast cancer, how she sought out the best specialists and was operated upon. When another tumour developed Eydie decided against further operations and with her husband she strenuously sought other possible cures. A visit to Ann Wigmore's Health Institute proved to be the turning point. Eydie Mae and her husband spent two weeks there learning how to grow and live with the new sprout and grass diet.

Eydie fasted on wheatgrass juice and then progressed to a regime of 'live food' – a mixture of uncooked sprouts, vegetables and separate fresh fruit meals. Maintaining this diet back home in California she was then able to control her cancer. Whenever she reverted to her previous diet the tumour began to grow again.

In Sweden more and more people try the live food alternative with sprouts to cure their illnesses usually after having tried all the conventional medicines and treatments offered by most medical doctors and public hospitals. Most health institutes of today have sprouts on their menu and the results they achieve are being more and more respected even to the point of attracting some researchers to devote some of their investigations to health food in relation to human well-being.

After all the attempts at traditional clinical cures had failed, Sigri Sahlin in Stockholm switched over to a diet of health foods including herbs, sprouts and grasses. All her life Sigri has been very vulnerable to infection, especially of the throat and vocal chords. Doctors diagnosed chronic asthmatic bronchitis and since her childhood she had also suffered severe joint pains. For all these symptoms she received masses of antibiotics, but they did not help. Now she is free from these troubles thanks to sprouts, herbs and general health foods. Even her severe periodic back pains have improved. But as soon as Sigri does not strictly adhere to her diet her problems return. At least a quarter of Sigri's food consists of grass and sprouts and in winter her intake of sprouts increases considerably as the available vegetables decline in quality and become so expensive. Sigri also eats many wild berries and herbs, which she picks herself in the environs of Stockholm.

In Japan the interest in sprouts and grasses is growing. For many years a religious community called Seicho-No-Ie have used wheatgrass therapies as a medicine for various illnesses with very good results. In Osaka, under the guidance of Dr Y. Hagiwara, extensive experiments have been performed even with dried grass both in the form of powder and tablets. Dr Hagiwara claims to have proved scientifically that grass even in this form is very wholesome and rich in nutrition. The powder, which is sold in Japanese health food stores, is mixed with water into a drink called green magma. In Sweden as well, grass and sprouts are sold in powdered forms. It is certainly better to use sprouts and grasses as live fresh food but probably it is better to use dried alternatives than no grass and sprouts at all.

Home-grown sprouts, ready for use

3
Sprouts in Children's Food

Many mothers wonder at what age infants can be given sprouts and in what form. There is no precise answer to this question as yet, since still so few infants have been given sprouts as part of their regular food, at least in modern Western society. No studies have been carried out in this field either.

There are, however, quite a number of families around the world with children that use sprouts and grasses as a significant part of their daily food. These children are usually first given alfalfa sprouts, often mixed with mashed potato. This sprout is mild and easily chewed and is also the most nutritious of the sprout species. After an introductory period with alfalfa it comes very naturally to introduce other sprouts, such as mung beans, lentils, wheat and fenugreek. They are all usually quickly accepted and very much enjoyed by most children.

In her books, Ann Wigmore also stresses the importance for expectant mothers to eat very healthy food with an abundance of sprouts and wheatgrass during their pregnancy. She also recommends mixing a teaspoonful of wheatgrass juice with the baby's food at an early stage and then successively increasing the quantity. As soon as the child moves on to solids, ground sprouts can be mixed into the food; finally, when the child starts chewing, the raw or parboiled sprouts can be included as they are.

Learning to grow sprouts and grasses is both fun and a useful pastime for children, whether at home or at school. They learn the importance of the daily careful attention to get good sprouts, acquiring at the same time a deep respect for living and growing nature.

It is exciting for them to see how the little dry seeds and beans quickly change into healthy living fresh sprouts and to watch how the tiny wheatgrass stalks have the strength of lifting up the paper covering placed on top of them.

Children also soon learn to remove the bad beans from the good ones and even this can become a game. They can begin growing their own sprouts in a special little glass jar. Another popular idea is to let them use a magnifying glass so that they can see what the sprouts and the dry beans look like in a larger perspective. This may also induce them to learn to distinguish the different kinds of sprouts from each other. A last piece of advice: give children sprouts instead of sweets and candies.

4
The Ecological Advantage of Sprouts

The wonderful thing about sprouts is not only that they are so nutritious but also that they are so extraordinarily cheap compared to the conventional processed food in our industrial society. If you use sprouts, grasses and herbs as a major part of your food, together with vegetables and fruit, you can cut down your food budget to a very low level. But even if you only treat sprouts as an extra, adding them to your usual health food intake or meat diet, you can still achieve significant savings. If you eat most of them uncooked you will do further savings on your energy bill by not using your oven.

Beans and seeds are so cheap that you can easily invest in building up a considerable storage of them in your pantry. Buying larger quantities usually also gives a better price, and few other foodstuffs keep as well and for such a long time as they do. Such a nutritional reserve is also an excellent insurance for future times when strikes or political problems might restrict the availability of foodstuffs.

Especially in the winter months, imported vegetables

are often of inferior quality and much more expensive due to long transports and high storage costs. To look fresh under all these conditions vegetables and fruits are usually heavily treated and sprayed and may even constitute a serious health risk. By comparison, home-grown and guaranteed untreated sprouts, sunflower seeds and wheatgrass are attractive, fresh and inexpensive alternatives.

The growing number of studies on the role of sprouts and grasses as alternative nutritional sources for mankind show that they are of vital importance for a realistic solution to the world's food problems. In many countries of the world man has largely been a vegetarian, which is really to cut one's coat according to one's cloth, since growing vegetables maximizes food production per acre compared to the space needed for meat production. With the spread of the Western way of life, there has been an increasing conversion to meat production based on the false assumption that meat contains better protein. This is foolish given the context of the protein deficiency. Soya beans and other protein rich crop varieties should therefore be encouraged. Even the National Academy of Sciences in the USA has come to the conclusion that our future protein requirements must come in much greater quantity from plant food and less from meat if we are going to survive.

The scarce acreage of the world suitable for cultivation must be used in both an economic and an ecological way. Ecology is good economy in the long run. Imagine also what an enormous contribution to cultivated acreage there would be if everyone the world over grew sprouts and grasses in their homes.

5
Check List for Beginners

1. *Buying*
Buy seeds and beans that have been treated as little as possible. Make sure they are for consumption and not seeding. It is a good idea to sprout a small sample directly after purchase to control the germination capacity.

2. *Storage of Seeds and Beans*
Seeds should be stored in dry, mild, dark conditions, especially if large quantities have been purchased. Label your seed jars, bags or sacks with date and purchase particulars.

3. *Pre-cleansing*
Pick out damaged, split or discoloured beans and other rubbish. Alfalfa and other very small seeds can be cleaned by rinsing them a couple of times before soaking, and skimming off the waste material which normally floats to the surface. Damaged seeds and beans remain hard even after lengthy soaking, and feel like small stones in the mouth.

4. Method

The method you use is a matter of personal taste and habit. Small seeds, especially those that form gelatine, grow best using the sprouter tray or plate method. Larger beans and even alfalfa are best suited to bottles, tubes, flowerpots, etc., because of the great increase in volume. Experiment and see which method best suits you and gives you good results.

5. Soaking

Soak the seeds in about four times as much water as the seed volume. Seeds and beans swell considerably in water. The gelatine-forming seeds do not need any soaking. In a sprouter, water percolates through the layers slowly enough for both the soaking and rinsing to be combined, so, if you use this method you need not soak, unless you want the sprouts to develop as quickly as possible.

Most beans and seeds can be soaked overnight. If you want to take a little more care, you can use the following rule of thumb. Large beans, such as lentils, garbanzo and aduki beans, as well as unhusked sunflower seeds and wheat grains, need a somewhat longer soaking period (12-15 hours), while small seeds like alfalfa, fenugreek, unhusked buckwheat, fennel and radishes can make do with a shorter period of soaking, say 6-8 hours. However, it does not really matter if these small seeds are soaked longer.

6. Rinsing

Rinsing may conveniently be done in the morning, before breakfast, and in the evening, before bed and, if necessary, one other time, for instance when coming home from work.

Some people recommend soaking and rinsing at room temperature or with softened water, but we have not noticed any difference when using cold tap water. The sprouts are exposed to fairly cold conditions in their natural state as well.

Make sure no water remains after rinsing, otherwise

CHECK LIST FOR BEGINNERS

the sprouts may go bad. Nor must they become too dry, or they soon wither and die. It is essential to have moisture during the whole sprouting period.

Do not shake the sprouts unnecessarily during rinsing. They are quite fragile and can easily be damaged by heavy handling. Sprouts that have split may turn bad. If you use the jar method you can hardly avoid shaking the sprouts to some extent while rinsing. They consequently become bent. With the flowerpot sprouter and paper towel methods, the sprouts all grow in the same direction and become straighter. However, crooked or straight, the nutritional value of the beans does not seem to be affected.

7. *Air Circulation*
It is very important for the sprouts to have access to air during growth. Make sure therefore that plastic bags, for example, are not so tight as to hinder air circulation.

8. *Growth Temperature*
Sprout normally develop well at room temperature. Soya beans and garbanzo prefer somewhat colder temperatures: the pantry for example. Be wary of cold draughts. Sprouts grow more quickly in warmer temperatures, more slowly in colder temperatures.

9. *Dark or Light Conditions*?
The fact that sprouts naturally grow in the dark suggests that this condition should be duplicated as much as possible. Put your sprouts in a kitchen cupboard or in the oven during the growing period. Experiments with sprouts that have stood constantly in light do not, in fact, show any obvious differences. However, research is being carried out as to what effect this may have on nutritional values. Vitamin B content, for example, seems to increase even more under dark growing conditions.

10. *Greening*
Place the grown sprouts on a windowsill or under a lamp. This leads to the formation of chlorophyll and even after a

few hours mild greening takes place. Remember, it is not advisable to put sprouts under direct sunlight, which can dry them out. Indirect sunlight or normal daylight are better. Even electric light does well. For a quicker greening, the sprouts can be spread out on a tray before being placed in light.

11. *Hulls*
Sprouts are usually eaten with their hulls intact. The nutritional value lost by taking off the hulls is probably insignificant but they contribute a good source of fibre, which the body certainly needs. Preferably the whole sprout, including the roots and leaves, should be eaten. The tough hulls of buckwheat sprouts should be removed. However, do not try to remove the hulls from the sprouts before they have become naturally loose, otherwise damage can occur and growth may be retarded.

12. *Final Cleansing*
If you forgot to clean the dry seeds, you now have another chance before serving. Place the sprouts in a colander or sieve and rinse, shaking gently. The sterile sprouts and other debris gravitate to the bottom and can be easily removed.

13. *Storage of Sprouts*
Ready-grown sprouts can be stored in the refrigerator where further growth is imperceptibly slow. They can be stored for up to a week without loosing their freshness. It is preferable, however, not to cultivate more than three to four days' supply at one time. Alfalfa sprouts do remain fresh for several days even if they are not put in the refrigerator. If you wish to preserve or deep-freeze sprouts they should be parboiled first.

Check List
If you are not successful with your sprouting, if the seeds do not grow or the sprouts dry out, rot, turn sour or mouldy or dry, then it may be for the following reasons:

CHECK LIST FOR BEGINNERS

- that you have obtained old, damaged or treated seeds or beans.
- that you have not cleansed them properly.
- that you have not rinsed them thoroughly.
- that several sprouts have broken and therefore begun to rot.
- that the sprouts have not been kept moist enough.
- that air circulation has been insufficient.
- that they have grown in too high, or too low temperature, or have been exposed to draught.
- that the vessel used was not properly cleaned.
- that the jar used was too small and the sprouts consequently too tightly packed together.

Begin with seeds and beans that are easy to sprout, such as alfalfa and mungbeans, and wait for soya beans and chick peas which require more care.

GOOD LUCK WITH YOUR SPROUTING!

Two tablespoonsful of seeds give a plateful of delicious alfalfa sprouts

6
Sprouting in Your Own Kitchen

Practical instructions, step by step
Pick out all damaged and discoloured seeds and any other rubbish. Then put the remaining seeds into a bottle with a wide neck.

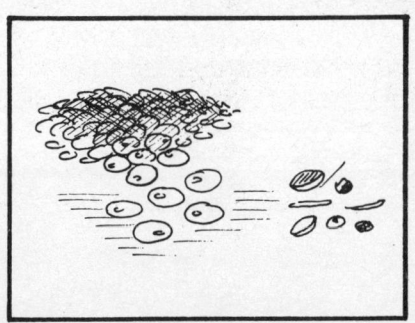

Cover the opening with a fine muslin. Fasten with a rubber band or string.

Rinse the seeds in running water.

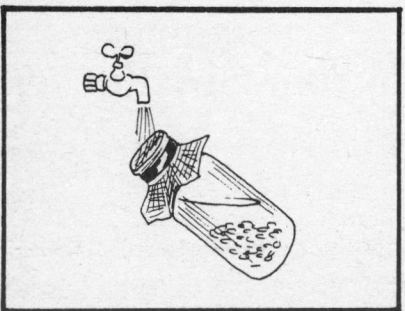

Soak the seeds overnight or for about twelve hours. Take one measure of seeds to four measures of water. Remember that some seeds swell more than others.

SPROUTING IN YOUR OWN KITCHEN

Pour away the water you soaked the seeds in and use it for your potted plants. Rinse the seeds once.

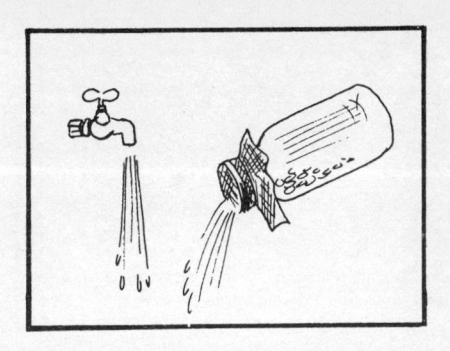

Angle the bottle so that excess water can run off and place it in a dark place at room temperature, a cupboard, for example.

Rinse the seeds two or three times daily. Some seeds may require even further rinsing. Note the instructions for the various seeds. Do not shake the bottle too much. Remember the sprouts are delicate.

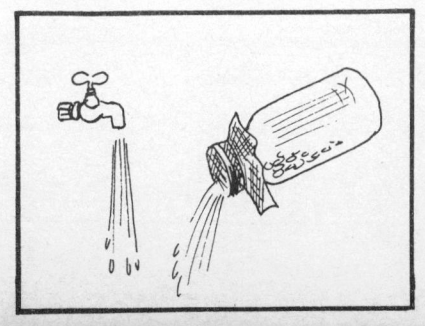

After three to five days the seeds are ready to be eaten. The ideal length of sprouting time given for each variety of seed should not be taken too literally. You can decide yourself when you want to eat your sprouts.

Stand the bottle on a windowsill for a few hours, or under a lamp, so that the tiny delicate leaves become green and create chlorophyll.

7
Sprouting Methods

JAR METHOD

Equipment: jars or wide necked bottles – for example, a one-litre fruit juice bottle. A fine mesh net – for example, cheesecloth, plastic mosquito netting or a nylon stocking. A rubber band or string.

This method has been previously described on pages 35-8. It is suitable for almost all types of sprouts, though not for those that form a jelly-like substance while sprouting, such as cress and mustard seed.

Using the jar method sprouts can be readily mixed together right from the start. For example mix mung beans, lentils and fenugreek; their growth rate is the same.

Jar Method

FLOWERPOT METHOD

Equipment: flowerpot of clay or plastic. Net or cheesecloth.

If you have an ordinary clay flowerpot, make sure it is properly cleaned. Brush out the inside and let the pot lie in clean water for a few hours to absorb moisture, otherwise the clay will draw away moisture from the needy sprouts.

Place the net in the bottom of the pot to prevent the beans from falling out. Fill up with soaked beans and cover the pot with a small plate.

Rinse two to four times daily by placing the flowerpot under the tape and pouring water over the sprouts. You can even transfer the sprouts into a colander to rinse them. If the sprouts turn mouldy in the flowerpot it is probably because it is still not quite clean. In this event, boil the pot in a saucepan for ten minutes.

Flowerpot Method

PLATE METHOD

Equipment: plate of stainless steel or china. Cling wrap, plastic sheet or towel.

The plate method is best suited for beans and seeds developing jelly while sprouting. Common cress is an example of this, as are radish and mustard seeds.

Spread the seeds out smoothly and fill with a similar amount of water. After one to two hours check whether more water is required or whether some excess water should be drained away. Water the seeds one or two times daily by spraying them with a hand shower or spray bottle.

Cover the plate with cling wrap in which you can make small air holes. The plastic holds the moisture. Put the plate away in a dark place. You can even place it in a dark bag, e.g. plastic bag, and leave the end open.

Plate Method

TOWEL METHOD

Equipment: glass, ceramic or stainless steel tray, wire cooling tray, grill rack or any other kind of metal grid. Two terry tea towels or paper towels.

Place the rack in the pan. Soak the towel in water, squeeze it and place it over the rack. Spread the soaked beans evenly over the towel. Cover them with the other, also dampened towel.

Method (a). Fill the pan with water so that the level reaches just under the rack. The bottom cloth remains wet as the underside lies in contact with the water (see diagram).

Make sure that the water level is maintained. Fill up with water once or twice a day. Ensure that even the top towel remains damp. Cover all with black plastic or place in darkness (e.g. in the oven).

Method (b). Do not pour water into the pan, but instead use a hand shower. Keep the beans moist by spraying them two or three times daily. Ensure that the top towel remains damp. Use black plastic as in Method (a).

Towel Method

SPROUTER METHOD

Equipment: sprouter (mini greenhouse).

Spread out a thin layer of beans on each tray. Soak them beforehand in a separate container if you wish to harvest them a day earlier. Fill up the top tray with ½ litre of room temperature water and put the lid on. The water should now percolate through the levels and collect in the draining tray at the bottom.

Water both morning and evening if possible. Place the sprouter in a dark cupboard during the first two days and then in a bright place for greening. Serve direct from the trays.

The sprouter is less suitable for beans which need rinsing several times a day, e.g. soya beans and chick peas. Sometimes the drainage outlets become blocked, especially with small seeds such as alfalfa and cress.

For those who simply want to eat sprouts as an 'extra' in their diet, the sprouter is adequate. If you want more sprouts, then other methods are better. The sprouter is perfect for children, as here they can really observe the whole growing process.

Sprouter Method

OTHER SPROUTING METHODS

New sprouters of different kinds are seeking patents in various parts of the world. The basic ideas, though, are always the same. There is a freedom for everyone to experiment with their own personal methods of growing. Choose methods with specific objectives in mind.

For large harvests and big kitchens the *bucket method* is the most practical. It works like the flowerpot method, but on a larger scale. Two plastic buckets are required, one slightly smaller than the other. Make small holes in the bottom of the larger bucket. Soak the seeds in the smaller bucket. Stretch a net or cheesecloth over the holes and transfer the seeds to the larger bucket, which is now placed in the smaller bucket (see illustration). Place a covering over the top of the bucket and keep them in room temperature.

In many countries, *the tube method* is also used. Plastic tubes are specially made for the purpose and have mesh masks or perforated lids at both ends. This method works either in the same way as the flowerpot method or you can let small sprouts such as alfalfa grow into a whole loaf, which can easily be pushed out in one piece.

In some books and newspaper articles, coffee, jam or honey jars are recommended, the lids having been perforated with holes. The problem with this method is that sometimes the sprouts do not get enough air and the holed tin lids rust. The run off after rinsing is not so efficient either.

The *sieve method* involves the sprouts being laid in a sieve or strainer to grow. The sieve is covered in the usual way, and rinsing becomes very easy.

In India a different *handtowel method* is used. The soaked seeds or beans are wrapped in a wet towel and left to sprout without any further rinsing. The sprouts are often used after only one day, or as soon as the small shoots first begin to appear.

Even *plastic (polythene) bags* can be used for sprouting. This method is suitable when there is a space problem, for example when travelling.

Place the seeds in a plastic bag and top up with three

times as much water. Allow the seeds to lie in the wet in the bag overnight. Take another plastic bag and puncture holes in it. Pour in the soaked seeds and shake out the water. Dampen a cloth or paper and wrap it around the sprout bag. Place all this in a larger plastic bag and fasten tight with a rubber band. Rinse the sprouts whenever an opportunity occurs, if you cannot do it regularly morning and evening.

8
Sprouting While Travelling

It is, in fact, not difficult to grow sprouts even when travelling. There are several handy 'portable' sprouting methods. Mungbeans, alfalfa and lentils are very suitable to use while travelling or trekking. If you stay at least a few days in the same hotel, you can, of course, sprout the same way as at home. Glass jars and bottles with wide necks can be obtained almost anywhere. All you have to remember is to take a fine net and some rubber bands with you. If for safety you take the bottles with you as well, choose plastic ones. They weigh less and do not break so easily. The tube method is also suitable for the traveller.

Of course, the person who cleans your hotel room is likely to be somewhat surprised at your sprouting equipment! Just explain to them what is going on and, most importantly, ask them not to shake the containers unnecessarily! Food preparation in hotel rooms does not always meet with the hotel manager's approval but sprouts look so clean and nice that there is generally no problem.

In hotels we usually put the sprout containers in the bath or basin, covering them with a dark cloth if necessary. One warning: be careful not to lose too many seeds down the plughole of the bath or basin since seeds swell considerably in water they might block it up.

Walkers, hitchhikers and others using rucksacks can also sprout while on the move. In this case, space being so restricted, it is perhaps easiest to use the plastic bag method.

Sprouts are a perfect food pack when climbing or trekking when you usually also have access to naturally pure mountain water.

When travelling abroad, it is important to know whether you are permitted by law to carry beans and seeds. In many countries it is in fact totally forbidden. Obtaining clean rinsing water can be a problem in tropical and other hot countries. In this event use distilled or boiled water which you filtrate with the help of carbon filters.

Mungbean sprouts

9
Sprout Directory

In the following sprout directory we give a short description of all the different kinds of sprouts used for our recipes. New types of seeds and beans suitable for sprouting are constantly popping up on the food market. Almost any viable seed can in fact be sprouted under proper conditions but seeds from tomato or potato should not be used for this purpose. They are poisonous.

As already mentioned comparatively little research has been done on the exact nutritional content of sprouts. The results presented in different literature may also vary considerably depending on at what stage of the sprouting process and under what conditions the tests have been carried out. Most of the nutritional values outlined in the directory concern dry seeds.

ADUKI BEANS

The little red aduki bean has been cultivated for centuries, in such regions as China, Japan and Korea. It is also sometimes called the red soya bean.

Aduki beans contain 25 per cent protein and all essential amino acids except tryptophan. The bean has also a high content of iron, niacin and calcium.

The taste is similar to that of mungbeans. Aduki beans can readily be an alternative to mungbeans in recipes.

Sprouting method: Bottle, flowerpot or tube
Soaking: About 12 hours
Rinsing: 4 times daily
Quantity: 1 measure beans gives 4 measures sprouts
Growing time: About 4 days
Ideal length: 3-4cm

ALFALFA

Alfalfa is used as animal fodder. The seed is known for its fantastic capability to penetrate deep into the soil for water. Alfalfa is one of the smallest sprouts, but it is superior to most others in nutritional value. No wonder it's called 'King of the sprouts' and even 'father of all foods'. The protein content of the seed is about 35 per cent.

Alfalfa sprouts contain all the most important vitamins and minerals. They contain as much carotene as carrots and they become especially rich in chlorophyll after greening.

The alfalfa sprouts are very mild and can be given to small children at an early age.

Alfalfa sprouts can be mixed into salads after only three days of growth. It is better, however, to wait until the leaves have started to develop and the chlorophyll has built up.

Sprouting method:	Bottle, sprouter or tube.
Soaking:	6-12 hours.
Rinsing:	2-3 times daily
Quantity:	1 measure seeds gives 10 measures sprouts
Growing time:	3 days for 1-2cm 6-7 days for 4-5cm
Ideal length:	3-4cm

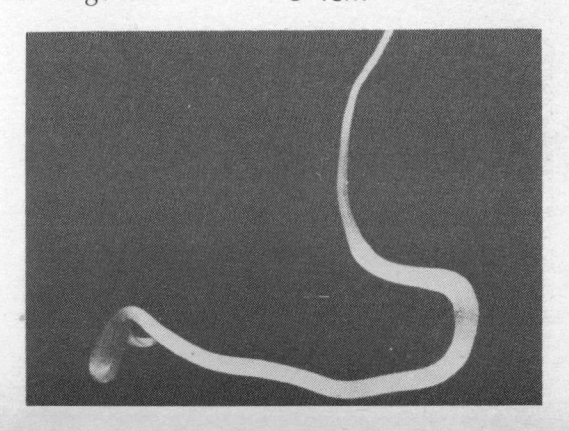

FENUGREEK

This 'greek hay' has become very popular as a sprout because of its unique taste. Fenugreek seeds are common constituents in curry mixtures.

Fenugreek has a 30 per cent protein content and is very rich in iron and vitamin A. The sprouts can be eaten after three days, but you can also wait until the leaves have developed after 5 days. The taste becomes somewhat more bitter if it grows too long.

Sprouting method:	Bottle, flowerpot or tube
Soaking:	12 hours
Rinsing:	2-3 times daily
Quanity:	1 measure seeds gives 8 measures sprouts
Growing time:	3-5 days
Ideal length:	3cm or 6cm with green leaves.

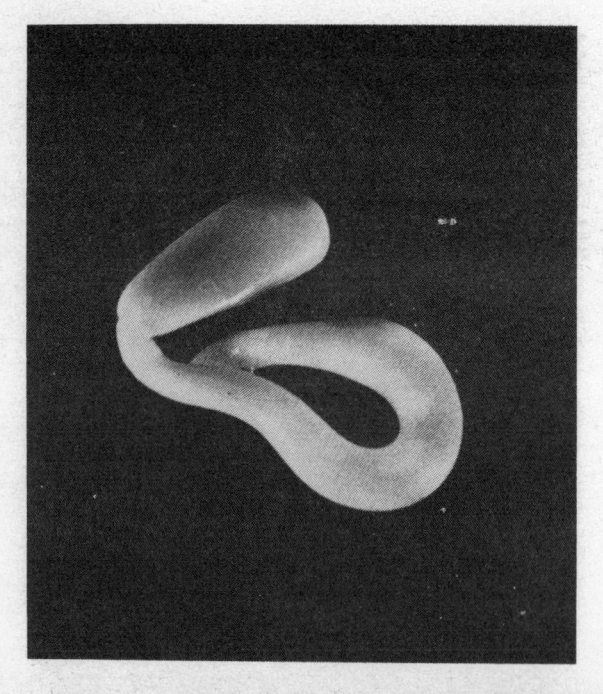

CHICKPEAS

Chickpeas, also called Garbanzo, are most common in Spain, Mexico, the Philippines and India. They are very drought-resistant and can be kept for years without endangering their viability. They are like yellow peas but have a more wrinkled surface.

Chickpeas contain about 20 per cent protein, vitamins A and C and iron, calcium and magnesium. Note that chickpeas swell a lot during soaking.

The sprouts need rinsing frequently and should preferably be eaten before they become more than 2-3cm long. Chickpeas turn mouldy more easily than other sprouts and should really not be grown together with other beans.

Like soyabeans, chickpeas should be quickly boiled in 3-5 minutes.

Sprouting method: Bottle or tube
Soaking: 12-18 hours
Rinsing: 3-5 times daily
Quantity: 1 measure peas gives 2 measures sprouts
Growing time: 2-3 days
Ideal length: 2-3cm

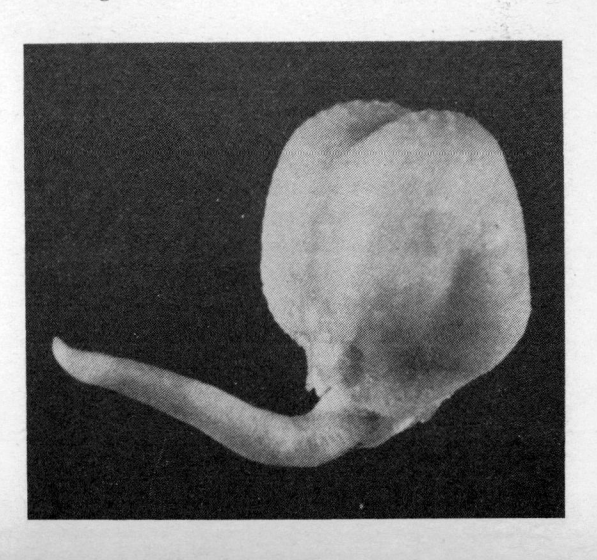

LENTILS

Lentils are associated by many with India, where they are used daily in cooking. Most common is the green-brown variety, though there are several kinds of different colour and size. All are easy to sprout as long as they still have their hulls.

The protein content of lentils is about 25 per cent. Vitamin C and E are increased significantly during sprouting. Other contents include Vitamins A and B and minerals, iron, phosporus and calcium.

Sprouting method: All methods
Soaking: 12 hours
Rinsing: 2-4 times daily
Quantity: 1 measure lentils gives 6 measures sprouts
Growing time: 3-4 days
Ideal length: 2-3cm

MUNGBEANS

Mungbeans are the most common sprouting beans. They are grown in many parts of the world, particularly in China, where they have been part of the traditional food for thousands of years.

Mungbeans contain 20 per cent protein, are rich in vitamins A, E and C and amino acids. Mungbean sprouts are edible after two days, although it is better to wait until the sprouts' two small leaves are visible. Mungbeans are good sprouts for beginners as they are very easy to grow.

Sprouting method: All methods
Soaking: 12 hours
Rinsing: 2-3 times daily
Quantity: 1 measure beans gives 4 measures sprouts
Growing time: 2-5 days
Ideal length: 2-4cm

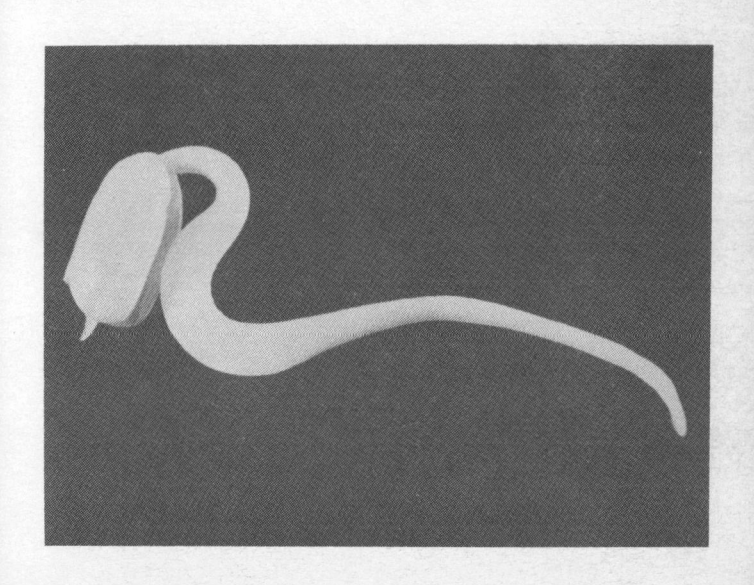

SOYABEANS

No other vegetable foodstuff has received so much attention in scientific literature as the soyabean. Already in 3000 BC, soyabeans were being used in the Orient. Then, much later, they cropped up in Europe, and now a cold-resistant variety is grown in Europe.

Soyabean sprouts are very rich in protein, nearly 40 per cent. They are also high in vitamin C and B and many minerals. Lecithin is extracted from soyabeans.

Soyabeans are fairly difficult to sprout. Be careful to pick away all damaged beans that show no sign of growth. It is important to rinse them 4-6 times daily, preferably every three hours. Soyabeans should be steamed or boiled for a few minutes before eating. This takes away most of the trypsin inhibitor which otherwise makes the soyabeans somewhat difficult to digest.

Sprouting method: Bottle, flowerpot or tube
Soaking: About 12 hours
Rinsing: 4-6 times daily
Growing time: 3-5 days
Quantity: 1 measure beans gives 4-5 measures sprouts
Ideal length: 2-4cm

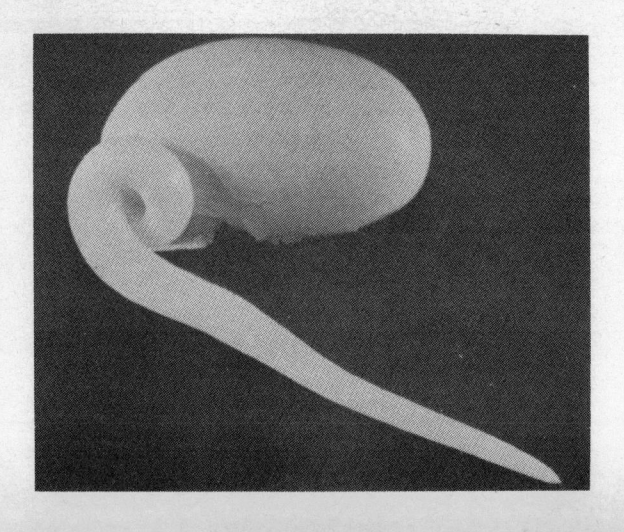

WHEAT

For the majority of the world's population, wheat is the most important source of nutrition. Each day over a billion people eat wheat in one form or another.

Sprouts from wheat contain 14 per cent protein and also calcium, phosphorus and iron, plus vitamins C, E and B, niacin, thiamine and pantothenic acid.

Wheat is easy to sprout. The small fluffy roots are sometimes mistaken for mould, but are quite natural and good to eat.

Barley, oats and rye are grown in the same way as wheat.

Sprouting method: All methods
Soaking: 12 hours
Rinsing: 2-3 times daily
Quantity: 1 measure wheat gives 3 measures sprouts
Growing time: 3-4 days
Ideal length: 2cm

PEAS

Peas have for a long time been a well known food source in Europe and they are also easy to sprout.

Peas contain about 20 per cent protein and the sprouts contain all essential amino acids and Vitamins C, B1 and A.

Pea sprouts add a tasty flavour to the salad reminiscent of freshly picked peas. The pea sprouts should not grow too long or they become slightly tough.

Growing method: Bottle or tube
Soaking: 12 hours
Rinsing: 3 times daily
Quantity: 1 measure peas gives 2 measures sprouts
Growing time: 3 days
Ideal length: 2cm

SPROUT DIRECTORY

The following seeds are also easy to sprout.

CRESS
You may already have tried growing water cress at home. Cress grows well in a sprouter or with the towel method.

BUCKWHEAT
Make sure you get *unhulled* buckwheat. Rinse the seeds, do not soak. Buckwheat sprouts are ready in two to three days. Rinse three or four times daily. Bottle, tube or towel method.

MILLET, SESAME AND RICE
Rinse seeds. Soak six to twelve hours. Grow in three to four days. Rinse two to four times daily. Ready to eat when the sprout is the same length as the seed. Bottle or sprouter method.

RADISH AND MUSTARD SEED
Rinse seeds. Do not soak. The sprouts are ready in three to four days. Rinse or spray two to four times daily. Radish and mustard sprouts are strong in taste and can be used as an extra spice in salads, etc. Sprouter or plate method.

Note
Do not sprout potato or tomato seeds, which are poisonous. In most health food shops you will find information about which seeds, other than those mentioned in this chapter, are good to sprout.

10

Wheatgrass and Sunflower Cultivation Indoors

'Do as cows do, eat grass', was the ironic headline in a weekly newspaper reporting Ann Wigmore's visit in Europe. The statement is not nearly as daft as it sounds. Recent research has shown that grass is a very suitable human food. Furthermore, if you cultivate it at home you can be sure the crop is unsprayed.

What is then so valuable about wheatgrass? Well, like sprouts, wheatgrass increases most of the nutritional substances during the first growth period. Thus the grass should be used from the seventh day of growth until it becomes 10-15cm in height.

Wheatgrass is one of the best sources of chlorophyll. Chlorophyll is a kind of synthesized sunlight that can be compared to the haemoglobin in our blood. The haemoglobin molecules have iron in their central atoms, whilst chlorophyll has magnesium. Certain animals even seem to be able to convert chlorophyll to haemoglobin in their bodies. This is why some scientists are so interested in its positive effects on our cells and our blood and sometimes call it 'concentrated sun power'.

A seed of grass does not contain any measurable amount of Vitamin C or carotene, but these substances are formed and greatly increased during grass growth. Furthermore, wheatgrass contains Vitamin E, riboflavin, thiamin and niacin, plus a long list of necessary minerals, e.g. zinc, which has been shown to be very important for pregnant women.

Sunflower seeds are also very healthy, easily cultivated and are handled in the same way as wheatgrass. You can use ordinary bird seeds for sunflower cultivation. Let the hulls on the leaves remain until they fall off naturally, otherwise the growth process may be impaired. Also make sure that your sunflower tray is replaced in the same position after watering and spraying or there may be a risk that the sunflower stalks will become entangled as they constantly turn their leaves towards the light.

Both wheatgrass and sunflower leaves taste delicious in salads and sandwiches. They can also be used to garnish a variety of dishes before serving. Both the stalks and the leaves of the sunflower plant should be eaten so as to fully assimilate the nutritional content. Wheatgrass and sunflowers are not merely for sick people but for everyone who wishes to remain healthy.

If you wish to cultivate wheatgrass and sunflowers according to the traditional lore, then you should grow them when the moon is full.

Ann Wigmore also deals with mulching in her books and underlines the importance of earthworms in the compost heap. Of course, to grow grass without worms or moonlight, and simply to sow new grass when the old is finished can give satisfactory results too!

HOW TO CULTIVATE WHEATGRASS

1. Use untreated wheat. Remove any damaged grain.
2. Soak the wheat for twelve to fifteen hours in three times its own volume of water.
3. Drain off the water and use it for your plants.
4. Take a deep-sided baking tray, flower pot or plastic tray and lay down a thin layer of moss or peat soil, about 1cm thick. Top this with about 2cm of ordinary soil. Try to obtain bio-dynamic soil that has not been artificially fertilised.
5. Spread out the seeds as evenly as possible over the soil surface.
6. Water with a can with a spray nozzle. Make sure the soil becomes thoroughly soaked.
7. Press the seeds down softly and carefully with a flat hand, so that they make proper contact with the soil. The seeds should lie on the soil surface so that the full length of grass can be harvested.
8. Cover with a layer of wet newspaper. If you want to prevent the seeds from coming into contact with the printed matter, you can put a thin layer of wet paper towels in between. Never use pages of colour print!
9. Cover over the newly seeded soil with black plastic of the type used for bin linings. This is to reduce water evaporation and to keep the seeds moist during the ensuing days.

Flower box   moss   soil

wheat   newspaper   plastic

10. Now allow the baking tray to stand for three days at room temperature. On the third day you will see the wheat shoots lift up the layer of newspapers. Remove the plastic and newspapers, water thoroughly and place the tray on the windowsill or in some other light place. During the next few days water both morning and evening. Do not water so much that the wheat stands in water. You can check the moisture by grasping a bunch of grass and thereby raising the whole bed.

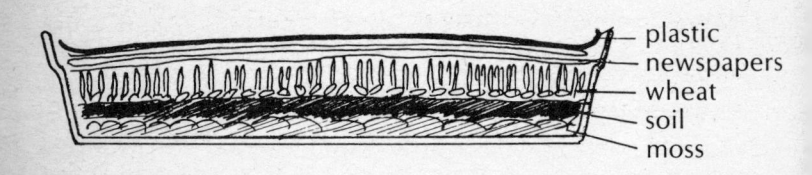

```
plastic
newspapers
wheat
soil
moss
```

11. After 7-8 days the grass will be 10-15cm high. It has become a deep green and can now be used. Cut with a sharp knife about 1cm above the soil surface (or use scissors). Finely chop the grass into salads or sandwiches. If you have a juicer you can make wheatgrass juice.
12. The cut grass can be kept in the refrigerator for about a week and still retains much of its nutritional value.
13. Water your wheatgrass tray again. You can obtain at least one or two further harvests.

You can also sow wheat without soil and grow grass. Ann Wigmore suggests that by growing in soil you obtain more of the minerals that the shoots take up.

The same principles can be used for the cultivation of sunflower 'grass'.

WHEATGRASS JUICE

From wheatgrass you can also obtain the chlorophyll-enriched wheatgrass juice that has become something of an elixir of life. Some even call it the 'survival cocktail'.

It is even used as an eye bath and as ear drops, though it must first be strained through a fine gauze. For an enema, add a full glass of wheatgrass juice to one litre of water. The grassy pulp that is left over after pressing can also be placed on sores and swellings to promote healing.

The best wheatgrass juice is obtained by using a special juicer (see photograph). This can also be attached to a motor, which should be set not to turn too fast. Wheatgrass is best ground down fairly slowly; the juice should not be allowed to become warm.

If you are unable to obtain a suitable juicer, you can use the berry or juice press attachment to any kitchen mixer – providing that the juicer is made of metal which can stand the heavy friction.

You can also prepare another wheatgrass drink by putting wheatgrass into a mixer/blender with a little water.

Sunflower grass or practically any grass at all will readily make a vitality-giving chlorophyll drink.

Wheatgrass hand-press

11
Practical Cooking Hints

RAW OR PARBOILED SPROUTS?
Now which is best and most wholesome? Raw or cooked sprouts? In the USA, fresh uncooked sprouts are most popular. In Chinese cooking they are nearly always served boiled or fried in oil. In India they are used in cooked and spiced combinations, but also raw, while in some other countries the whole thing has become rather a matter of dispute. No one would however think of parboiling lettuce or watercress. And doesn't it in the same way seem most natural and wholesome to eat alfalfa sprouts fresh?

We certainly can treat sprouts with heat, as long as we do it in a gentle way. Sprouts, especially from larger beans, benefit from quick cooking. But sprouts never need the long cooking which ordinary beans demand. Light boiling for a few minutes is well enough, although soya bean sprouts could well be cooked for five to ten minutes. Only part of the vitamin value is destroyed in such short cooking times, and meanwhile the proteins are made more usable for the body.

If you are a confirmed raw food eater, then moderate amounts of all kinds of fresh sprouts will do you good. At some of the health institutes in the USA serving a sprout-centred raw food diet, they have even thrown out the cooker, or at least stowed it in a corner. They do no cooking or frying at all.

Don't grow too many sprouts at once! Many beginners get worried because they find they cannot eat all the sprouts they have grown. Often sprouts grow more and faster than one would think. So even though they can keep well in the refrigerator for up to a week, do not grow more than you need for about two or three days at a time. If, even then, there are some sprouts left, and you cannot find the time or the enthusiasm to invite some friends round for dinner, you can use them amongst mixed vegetables or in soups. Just remember to add them at the end of the cooking. You can also use left-over sprouts in vegetarian rissoles or sproutburgers, which you can then store in deep freeze. Fresh sprouts should never be frozen, but they do keep well in the refrigerator.

The length of sprouts is also important if you want to eat them fresh, both for the sake of taste and texture. They can easily become stale and bitter in taste and lose their crispy crunchy freshness if they grow too long. They are more appetizing in that case if you boil them with cooked mixed vegetables, or in soups or minces. But do not treat people to old sprouts under any circumstances! You will ruin their good reputation.

Also make sure the sprouts do not get mouldy, sour or dried out. If you suspect they have gone bad, you should throw the whole lot away. If the top layer has dried out a bit, throw it away and use the rest with confidence. But it is seldom that sprouts go bad. Soya sprouts can sometimes go sour if you fail to rinse them regularly enough. If nevertheless you fail to sprout well, look at the checklist on page 29.

The hulls on sprouts have little nutritional value, but they are good for the stomach since they are rich in fibre. So eat sprouts whole, hulls and all.

The special green leaf of the smaller sprouts such as

alfalfa, fenugreek, wheat and cress give very good results. They can become really dark green.

VARIETY GIVES PLEASURE

You will manage any surprise visits in royal fashion if you have sprouts at home. Think of all the imaginative and different sandwiches and snacks you could rustle up! Anything from alfalfa seeds which didn't sprout to tasty sproutburgers or crunchy salads.

12
Sprout Recipes

PLATES OF RAW VEGETABLE DISHES

Place decorative piles of vegetables directly on to each plate. Then cover with finely-chopped parsley, chives or wheatgrass.

Boiled potatoes, especially with a knob of butter, are an excellent compliment.

Here are four seasonal raw vegetable dishes:

Summer Plate

Sprouts of your choice
Tender dandelion leaves
Lettuce
Sliced white cabbage
Fresh onion
Sliced radishes
Sliced tomatoes

Autumn Plate

Alfalfa sprouts
Mungbean sprouts
Coarsely-chopped carrots
Coarsely-chopped beetroot
Endive lettuce
Tomato slices
Cucumber slices
Cauliflower florets

Winter Plate

Alfalfa sprouts
Lentil sprouts
Chickpea sprouts, boiled
Grated carrots
Grated beetroot
Quartered tomatoes
Green pepper slices
Chopped avocado
Chopped mushrooms

Spring Plate

Alfalfa sprouts
Mungbean sprouts
Lentil sprouts
Chickpea sprouts, boiled
Grated carrots
Grated beetroots
Finely-chopped onion in yogurt
Quartered tomatoes
Green pepper rings

SPROUTS WITH HOT DISHES

Rice Grotto

2 cupsful of mixed sprouts
Cheese slices
$\frac{1}{2}$ cupful brown rice
Quartered tomatoes
Cucumber slices
Green pepper rings
Soysauce
Sesame salt
Butter
Lettuce

Boil the rice (40 minutes) and season with the soysauce. Cut up the vegetables into different, decorative pieces and display the portions in the following way:

Place some lettuce leaves around the plate. Then position the sprouts and vegetables in a broad decorative ring on the plate, leaving a substantial opening in the centre. Press the cheese slices into this opening, and then fill up with the heated rice. Top with a knob of butter. Sprinkle the whole dish with sesame salt.

Bean Grotto

Exchange the rice of the previous recipe for a tin of baked beans in tomato sauce. If you have time, we recommend using some soyabean sprouts or chickpea sprouts instead (parboiled for 10 minutes). Add tomato sauce and a dash of soysauce.

Mashed Potato Grotto

As above, but with mashed potato instead of rice. Recommended as a good alternative for small children. Divide up the different sorts of sprouts with slices of green pepper, as children usually enjoy learning to recognize the different sprouts.

SALADS

Budget Salad

1 cupful fenugreek sprouts
1 cupful lentil sprouts
1 cupful nettle sprouts
$\frac{1}{2}$ cupful spruce shoots or dandelion leaves
10-15 sunflower shoots
$1\frac{1}{4}$ cupsful red cabbage
Kelp
Additional choice:
Parboiled chickpea sprouts
Crushed nuts

Chop the nettle and spruce shoots (or dandelion leaves) finely. Shred or grate the red cabbage and mix all the ingredients thoroughly. Lightly powder with a little kelp.

If you wish to increase the protein content and stretch your budget salad to make a whole meal, then add parboiled chickpea sprouts or crushed nuts and serve with a cheese sandwich.

Everyday Salad

1 cupful alfalfa sprouts
1 cupful mungbean sprouts
$\frac{1}{2}$ crown lettuce
$\frac{1}{2}$ cucumber
2 medium-sized tomatoes
Chives/parsley

Place the lettuce leaves around the edge of the plate. Slice the cucumber and quarter the tomatoes. Mix the sprouts and cucumber and garnish with the tomatoes. Sprinkle chives and parsley over the top.

Protein Salad

- 1 cupful parboiled chickpea sprouts
- 1 cupful parboiled soyabean sprouts
- $\frac{1}{2}$ cupful alfalfa sprouts
- 1 avocado
- 1 cupful of cottage cheese
- 2 tablespoonsful crushed cashew nuts
- 1 tablespoonful kelp/herb salt

Cut the avocado in half, take out the stone and scoop out the flesh with a spoon. Add the parboiled sprouts, which should be allowed to cool before they are mixed into the salad. Mix all the ingredients together and sprinkle the cashew nuts on top. Serve with Sunflower Dressing.

Triplet Salad

- 1 cupful alfalfa sprouts
- 1 cupful mungbean sprouts
- 1 cupful lentil sprouts
- $\frac{1}{2}$ cupful fennel
- $\frac{1}{2}$ cupful coarsely-grated beetroot
- $\frac{1}{2}$ cupful diced courgette

Mix together thoroughly and finally add the grated beetroot, together with a little oil.

Sweetcorn Salad

- $1\frac{1}{2}$ cupsful alfalfa sprouts
- 1 tin of sweetcorn
- $\frac{1}{2}$ cucumber
- 1 red pepper

Dice the cucumber and mix in the alfalfa sprouts and the sweetcorn. Garnish with rings of red pepper.

Cauliflower Salad

½ cauliflower
2 cupsful of sprouts
⅓ leek
1 pepper

Break up the head of the cauliflower into small chewable florets. Chop up the leek and the pepper. Mix all the ingredients together and serve with an avocado dressing.

Potato Salad

1 cupful fenugreek sprouts
1 cupful aduki bean sprouts
4 medium-sized boiled potatoes
1 small leek
1¼ cupsful of yogurt or sour cream
Kelp/herb salt
Chives

Cube the potatoes and slice the leek. Stir in 1-2 teaspoonsful of kelp into the yogurt or sour cream and pour this over the potatoes and the leek. Mix in the sprouts. Sprinkle with some finely-chopped chives. Serve chilled.

Red Cabbage Salad

1¼ cupsful alfalfa sprouts
2 cupsful finely-chopped red cabbage
¾ cupful yogurt or sour milk
1 shredded pepper
Sage

Stir the red cabbage into the yogurt or sour milk. Spice the alfalfa sprouts and lay them over the red cabbage as a cover. Garnish with shreds of pepper.

Pizza Salad

- ¼ white cabbage
- 1¼ cupsful mungbean sprouts
- ½ red pepper
- 1 carrot
- 1 teaspoonful grated horseradish
- Olive oil
- Herb salt

Shred the cabbage and coarsely grate the carrot. Use long straight mungbean sprouts grown by the flower-pot method. Slice the pepper into lengths and mix up all the ingredients. Spice and add oil to taste.

Cheese Salad

- 1 cupful fenugreek sprouts
- 1 cupful alfalfa sprouts
- 1 cupful cheese cubes
- ½ cupful of blue cheese
- ¾ cupful finely-chopped fennel
- ½ pepper

Chop up the pepper and mix it with the other ingredients. Crumble the blue cheese over the salad.

Fetta Cheese Salad

- 1 cupful alfalfa sprouts
- 1 cupful mungbean sprouts
- 100g (4 oz.) fetta cheese
- ½ crown lettuce
- ½ red pepper
- 10 mushrooms
- 2 tomatoes
- ¼ cucumber
- 1 tablespoonful of olive oil

Cut up the vegetables into small pieces. Mix together thoroughly with the sprouts and the oil, and crumble the fetta cheese over the salad.

DRESSINGS

Avocado Dressing

1 avocado
1 cupful water
1 cupful cashew nuts
1 teaspoonful kelp

Halve the avocado and remove the stone. Scoop out the flesh and place this in a blender. Add the water, nuts and kelp. Blend together until a fairly thick consistency is obtained. Place in the refrigerator and serve cold with salads.

Sunflower Dressing

$1\frac{1}{2}$ cupsful hulled sunflower seeds
1 small chopped beetroot
1-2 cupsful water
1 teaspoonful herb salt or kelp

Mix the sunflower seeds and beetroot in water. Add the herb salt or kelp. Regulate the water quantity so that the dressing becomes thick but flows freely. The beetroot gives the dressing a rich pink colour.

Sesame Dressing

$\frac{1}{2}$-$\frac{3}{4}$ cupful hulled sesame seeds
$\frac{1}{2}$ cupful water
$\frac{1}{4}$ cucumber
2 tablespoonsful lemon juice
1 tablespoonful kelp

Mix the sesame seeds with the cucumber and the kelp in the water. Lace with lemon juice.

Honey Dressing

Yogurt
Honey

Add one teaspoonful of honey to a cupful of yogurt. If the honey is thick, mix it first with a little warm water. Serve with a sprout salad. Lessen the honey content if you think it too sweet.

Herb Dressing

$\frac{1}{4}$ cupful olive oil
$\frac{1}{2}$ cupful sesame oil
$\frac{1}{4}$ cupful lemon juice
1 crushed garlic clove
$\frac{1}{2}$ teaspoonful chopped parsley
$\frac{1}{2}$ teaspoonful oregano
$\frac{1}{2}$ teaspoonful dill
$\frac{1}{2}$ teaspoonful basil

Stir the oils together with the lemon juice. Add the garlic and the herbs. Shake the mixture well and serve with sprout salads.

SANDWICHES

Vitamin Sandwich

1 slice wholemeal bread
Butter
1 pepper
Alfalfa sprouts
Tomato
Cress
Lettuce leaves

Butter the bread sparingly. Cover with some lettuce leaves, then a layer of alfalfa sprouts and a ring of pepper. Garnish with tomato slices and finely-cut cress.

Sweetheart Sandwich

1 slice wholemeal bread
Butter
Fenugreek sprouts
Red pepper

Butter the bread and cover with the fenugreek sprouts. Cut out a heart of red pepper and place on top of the sprouts.

Royal Yacht Britannia

½ bread roll
Butter
Cottage cheese
Lentil sprouts
Pepper shreds
1 leaf of Chinese cabbage

Butter the bread and spread on the cottage cheese. Cut out shreds from the pepper and use as 'railings' round the bread. Fill with lentil sprouts as small 'sailors'. Cut a sail out of the Chinese cabbage leaf and stick it in the 'hull' of bread. A dash of sea salt gives this sandwich the tang of a sailor's life!

Ship Ahoy Sandwich

½ roll of rye bread
Butter
Vegetable paste
Alfalfa sprouts
1 leaf of Chinese cabbage

Spread the butter thinly over the roll of bread and then the vegetable paste. Add a generous handful of alfalfa sprouts to cover the whole sandwich. Cut out a sail from the Chinese cabbage and stick it in the centre of the bread.

Royal Yacht Britannia

A sprout picnic

A simple sprout meal

Party Loaf

1 loaf of wholemeal bread
Butter
Cheese slices
Vegetable paste
Alfalfa sprouts
Fenugreek sprouts
Lentil sprouts
Tomato slices
Cucumber slices

Slice the loaf without cutting right through to the bottom. Butter the insides of every second cut and then cover the buttered sides, alternating with the cheese slices and the vegetable paste. Add the tomato, the cucumber and the sprouts in the same cuts. Serve the loaf as it is and let the guests cut off their own sandwich. Alternatively, warm the whole loaf in the oven for about 2 minutes at 200°C (400°F, Gas Mark 5).

Sprout Sandwich With Mushrooms

1 slice wholemeal bread
Butter
Mungbean sprouts
Sliced mushrooms

Spread butter on the bread. Put on the sprouts and chopped mushrooms. Sprinkle with finely cut parsley and knob of garlic butter. Top it with a couple of slices of cheese and sprinkle with a little paprika powder. Heat in oven for 5-10 minutes at 250°-275°C (482-500°F, Gas Mark 8), or place under the grill.

Mini Pizza

1 bap
Butter
Sprouts
1 tomato
1 tablespoonful chopped onion
Cheese slices
Kelp powder/herb salt

Cup the bap in two thin round slices and then butter. Season with oregano. Add the onion and thinly-sliced tomato. Cover with cheese slices. Place in the oven for 5-10 minutes at 250°C (482°F, Gas Mark 8), or under the grill.

SPROUT SPECIALS
Alfalfa Loaf

Use a glass or a plastic tube for sprouting. It should be open at both ends, otherwise it is impossible to remove the sprout loaf in one piece. The tube should be about 15-20cm long and have a diameter of about 10cm.

First place 50g (2 oz. or about 5-6 dessertspoonsful) of alfalfa seeds to soak in a glass bottle or jar overnight. Then transfer them to the tube and rinse them two or three times daily. After four or five days the tube will be filled with sprouts. If they start to bulge out from the ends, pull out a handful to allow a little more room. Finally, place the tube under a lamp on a window-sill for a further two days. The sprouts will then become a healthy green colour and be full of chlorophyll. Turn the tube now and again so that the light reaches all the leaves.

Push out the compact growth of sprouts in one whole piece and put the 'loaf' on a cutting board. It can now be cut into slices to make interesting snacks, or it can be left whole to form the centre-piece of a meal with a variety of other sprouts and vegetables placed around it.

If, instead of slicing the loaf, you just pull out tufts as required, then it will last longer. If you cut the loaf with a knife, remember to put the remainder into the refrigerator straight away.

Slices from the alfalfa loaf can either compliment a dish with raw vegetables or they can be served in the following ways:

1. Over or under a vegetarian burger.
2. As a middle ingredient of a sprout burger, or a double-decker (club) sandwich.
3. As an ingredient of the 'Party Loaf' (see page 91).
4. As the base of a gratin.

Big Mac Special

1 large rye bread roll
½ cupful mungbean sprouts
½ cupful of alfalfa sprouts
Tomato slices
Mushrooms
Cheese
Vegetable Paste
Butter

Cut the roll into three slices. Spread a little butter on the lower two slices and some vegetable paste on the third. Put a layer of mungbean sprouts and some slices of cheese between the two bottom slices. Place the alfalfa sprouts, slices of mushroom and of tomato on the upper one. Cover with the top slice.

Mini Burger

1 small bread roll
Alfalfa sprouts
Tomato
Vegetable paste
Butter

Cut the bread into two halves. Spread with butter and vegetable paste on both halves and garnish with tomato slices and a generous portion of alfalfa sprouts.

Sprout Burger

1 wholemeal roll
Butter
Alfalfa sprouts
Mungbean sprouts
Mustard seed sprouts
4-5 sunflower shoots
1 sprout rissole (see page 120)
Onion
Tomato
Cheese

Halve the bread and lightly butter it. Cover with some onion rings and mustard seed sprouts followed by a layer of mungbean sprouts and a hot sprout rissole. Then cover with a cheese slice, some tomato slices and some alfalfa sprouts. Stick in the sunflower shoots and top with the other half slice. Serve at once.

Potato Burger

1 wholemeal roll
$\frac{1}{4}$ cupful of mashed potato
1 sprout rissole
Alfalfa sprouts

Halve the roll and place warm mashed potatoes on both with the warm rissole and alfalfa sprouts in between.

Sprout burger

Sprout Tube

Soft flat bread (e.g. pitta bread)
Alfalfa sprouts
Parboiled chickpea sprouts
Hot potatoes
Tomato
Cucumber
Onion or garlic
Herb salt
Butter
Cheese

Butter the bread. Mash the warm potatoes together with the chickpea sprouts and spread over the bread. Leave some of the buttered surface uncovered so that it can be rolled together. Thinly slice the tomato, cucumber and onion and place them on top of the potato. Cover with alfalfa sprouts and a thin slice of cheese. Season with herb salt. Roll the bread to form a tube and eat while the potato is still hot.

Sprout Pocket

If you have real pitta bread with a pocket, put your sprout filling into the pocket.

STUFFED VEGETABLES

Avocado With Cottage Cheese

1 medium-sized avocado
½ cupful alfalfa sprouts
Cottage cheese
1 pepper
Herb salt/kelp powder

Mix the alfalfa sprouts with the cottage cheese and add a little sour cream if the cheese is too dry. Stir in a little finely-chopped pepper. Season with herb salt or kelp powder. If you want a stronger taste add a little garlic to the cottage cheese. Halve the avocado and carefully remove the stone, and then fill the cavity with the cheese mixture. This can be served as an entrée dish or with a salad.

Sprout Canoe

1 medium-sized cucumber
Alfalfa sprouts
Cottage cheese
Sour cream
Onion
Garlic
Herb Salt

Cut the cucumber in half lengthwise. Scoop out the middle flesh and mix it with the cottage cheese, a little sour cream, alfalfa sprouts and finely-chopped onion. Season with garlic and herb salt to taste. Place the sprout canoe on the table and let the guests cut their pieces themselves. You can also place the canoe on a bed of alfalfa sprouts.

Stuffed Tomatoes

4 medium-sized tomatoes
$\frac{1}{4}$ cupful alfalfa sprouts
$\frac{1}{4}$ cupful mungbean sprouts
$\frac{1}{4}$ cupful lentil sprouts
Cottage cheese
Kelp powder
Parsley/wheatgrass

Cut off the top of the tomatoes and scoop them out with a spoon (save the flesh for soups, etc.). Finely chop the sprouts and mix them with the cottage cheese. Stir in chopped garlic and add kelp powder to taste. Fill the tomatoes with this mixture. Garnish with finely-cut parsley or wheat grass. Serve as a starter or with salads and hot dishes.

Stuffed Peppers

2 large peppers
1 cupful parboiled chickpea sprouts
$\frac{1}{2}$ cupful lentil sprouts
$\frac{1}{2}$ cupful fenugreek sprouts
2 small tomatoes
$\frac{1}{2}$ onion
1 tablespoonful soysauce
1-2 teaspoonsful kelp powder
Cheese slices

Cut off the tops of the peppers and take out the contents. Put the chickpea sprouts, tomatoes and onion into a blender. Blend the mixture with the sprouts and add the kelp powder and soysauce. Fill the peppers with this mixture and top with cheese. Heat in an oven for 10 minutes at 250°C (482°F, Gas Mark 8), or until the cheese turns golden yellow.

OTHER STUFFINGS

3-4 cupsful of sprout rissole mix (see page 120)

If you are in a hurry you can use ready-made vegetable mixes.

- $\frac{1}{2}$ packet ready-made vegetable mix
- $\frac{3}{4}$ cupful water
- 1-1$\frac{1}{2}$ cupsful sprouts
- 2 tablespoonsful chopped onion
- Cheese

Place the sprouts and water in a blender. Blend in the ready-made vegetable mix and the onion, and then fill the peppers. Cover with one or two cheese slices and place in the oven for about 15 minutes at 250°C (482°F, Gas Mark 8).

Courgettes With Sprouts

- 1 medium-sized courgette
- 1 cupful lentil sprouts
- $\frac{1}{2}$ cupful mushrooms
- $\frac{1}{2}$ onion
- 1 tomato
- 2 tablespoonsful olive oil
- 2 tablespoonsful grated cheese
- 1 clove of garlic
- Herb salt

Cut off a lid along the length of a whole courgette. Scoop out the contents and chop this together with the onion, mushrooms and tomato. *Sauté* the mixture in the olive oil, together with the sprouts. Season, and then fill the two courgette halves with the mixture. Place them on a well-buttered oven-proof dish and sprinkle with the grated cheese. Add a knob of butter on top and place in the oven for 20-25 minutes at 250°C (482°F, Gas Mark 8).

Dolmades

4 medium-sized cabbage leaves
1 cupful sprouted rice
¾ cupful water
¾ cupful lentil sprouts
½ cupful fenugreek sprouts
2 medium-sized boiled potatoes
1 onion
1 teaspoonful marjoram
1 teaspoonful paprika powder
Herb salt
Soysauce
1 vegetable stock cube

Parboil the cabbage leaves for about 5 minutes. Cook the sprouted rice for ten minutes. Drain, but save the liquid. Grate or chop up the sprouts, potatoes and onion, and mix this together with the rice. Place the rice and sprout mixture on to the 4 cabbage leaves, roll up and then press together. Put the dolmades in a saucepan. Mix together the rice water, soysauce and the stock cube and pour over the dolmades. Cook for 5-15 minutes, depending on the thickness of the dolmades. Browning them with a little butter will give a richer taste and a golden colour.

Cannelloni

10-12 cannelloni
2 tablespoonsful olive oil
2 litres of water
Filling:
2½ cupsful sprouts
1 tablespoonful soysauce
½ cupful cottage cheese
2 tablespoonsful nutmeg
Herb salt

Sauce:
1 tin of tomatoes
2 onions, chopped
1-2 cloves of garlic
1 teaspoonful paprika powder
1 teaspoonful basil
Kelp powder

Boil the water together with the olive oil. Put in 5 cannelloni at a time and let them boil for 4-5 minutes.

Filling: Chop the vegetables and mix them thoroughly with the cottage cheese. Season with soysauce and herb salt.

Sauce: Boil the tomatoes and onions for 5 minutes. Season to taste. Fill the cannelloni with the help of a knife or a small spoon. Place in a well-buttered oven-proof dish. Pour the sauce over and sprinkle with grated cheese. Heat for 20 minutes at 200°C (425°F, Gas Mark 7).

Alternative filling: See Sprout Balls and Sprout Rissoles (pp. 120 and 121). Fill with the mixture and follow the recipe above.

Filled Pancakes

3 cupsful flour
1 cupful buckwheat flour
1 cupful wholemeal flour
9 cupsful milk
Margarine or oil

Mix the different flours with 4 cupsful of milk and whisk it even. Pour in the rest of the milk. Allow the mixture to stand for about an hour before frying the pancakes in oil or margarine over a low heat. Place one pancake on the plate, cover half with the filling, fold the other half over or form it into a tube.

SUGGESTED FILLINGS:
1. Stewed spinach with mungbean sprouts.
2. Parboiled, finely-chopped green cabbage and lentil sprouts.
3. Mixed vegetables, *sautéed* in a little oil. Add alfalfa sprouts and vegetable mix when filling the pancake.
4. Your choice of salad with sprouts.

PIZZAS

Simple Pizza Dough (2 persons)

3 cupsful white flour
1½ cupsful warm water
25g (1 oz.) yeast
1 tablespoonful olive oil

Stir in the yeast thoroughly with the water so that no lumps are left. Pour in the flour and oil and knead or beat the dough together. Allow it to rise for about 30 minutes in a warm place. Divide the dough in two and knead out two thin cakes. Place these on a plate and sprinkle with flour. Fold up the edges and spread out the pizza filling. Bake for 10 minutes at 275°C (500°F, Gas Mark 8). It is also possible to use ready-made, soft, flat bread (or pitta bread) as the pizza base.

PIZZA FILLINGS

Choose proportions of the following ingredients to suit your personal taste.

Funghi

Lentil sprouts
Fenugreek sprouts
Whole mushrooms
Onion
Crushed tomatoes
Cheese
Brewer's Yeast
Oregano
Herb salt

Sprinkle oregano on the uncovered pizza dough. Pour on the crushed tomatoes and spread with the sprouts and mushrooms. Chop the onions and sprinkle over the mixture. Dust with a little herb salt and the yeast and cover with cheese slices. Bake for 10-15 minutes at 275°C (500°F, Gas Mark 8).

Quattro Stagione Pizza

Mungbean sprouts
Lentil sprouts
Fenugreek sprouts
Aduki bean sprouts
1 pepper
Mashed tomatoes
Artichoke hearts
Cheese
Oregano

Sprinkle oregano over the uncovered pizza dough. Pour on the crushed tomatoes. Place one artichoke heart in the middle of each pizza. Shred the pepper and use the strips to divide up the pizza into four sections. Place one variety of sprouts in each quarter and cover with cheese slices. Bake for 10-15 minutes at 275°C (500°F, Gas Mark 8).

Calzone

1 cupful alfalfa sprouts
1 cupful lentil sprouts
1 cupful mungbean sprouts
1 pepper
3 tomatoes
100g (4 oz.) grated cheese
1 teaspoonful oregano
1 teaspoonful basil

Shred the pepper finely, mash the tomatoes and mix together with the sprouts. Stir in the cheese and the seasonings. Roll out the pizza dough and spread the mixture as a wide band in the middle of the dough. Fold over the edges so that they meet in the middle and pinch into a pattern. Finish off by making a twist at each end. Bake for 10-15 minutes at 275°C (500°F, Gas Mark 8).

GRATINS

Celeriac Gratin

1 stick of celeriac
1 chopped onion
1 sliced tomato
2 tablespoonsful wheat flour
2 tablespoonsful olive oil
$\frac{1}{4}$ cupful cream
$\frac{3}{4}$ cupful water
Soysauce
Herb Salt
$\frac{3}{4}$-1 cupful grated cheese
Stewed Sprouts:
1 cupful lentil sprouts
1 cupful fenugreek

Peel the celeriac and cut into slices (about 1cm thick). Boil for 5-10 minutes and put them packed together in an oven-proof dish. Lightly fry the sprouts and onions in oil. Sprinkle on the flour and add a little water and cream. Let the mixture simmer gently on a low heat for 5-10 minutes. Season with soysauce and herb salt. Pour the whole mixture over the celeriac slices, place the tomato slices on top, and finally cover with grated cheese. Bake in the oven for about 20 minutes at 275°C (500°F, Gas Mark 8).

Cauliflower Gratin

½ cauliflower
1 cupful mungbean sprouts
½ cupful lentil sprouts
1 small packet of chopped spinach
¾ cupful cream
1 chopped onion
1 teaspoonful soysauce
2 tablespoonsful oil
Herb salt
Cheese slices

Break up the cauliflower into small florets. Boil until they are almost soft. Place them in an ovenproof dish. *Sauté* the onion and sprouts in oil. Pour on the spinach and stir in the cream. Season with soysauce and salt. Pour the spinach mixture over the cauliflower and cover with the cheese slices. Bake in the oven for 20 minutes at 275°C (500°F, Gas Mark 8).

SOUPS

Yellow Pea Soup

2 cupsful yellow pea sprouts
1 litre (1¾ pt.) water
1 chopped onion
1 sliced carrot
1 crushed garlic clove
1 teaspoonful vegetable bouillon paste
Thyme/marjoram

Dissolve the vegetable paste in 800ml of hot water. Add the onion and carrot slices and boil for five minutes. Stir in half the pea sprouts and boil for another five minutes. Mix the remaining pea sprouts with 200ml of water in a blender for 15 seconds. Add this mixture to the soup and bring to the boil. The soup is now ready to be served. Season with thyme or marjoram to taste. This soup has a genuine flavour of fresh peas.

Green Pea Purée

2 cupsful green pea sprouts
1 litre (1¾ pt.) water
1 chopped onion
Herb salt
Vegetable bouillon paste

Parboil the sprouts for five minutes in 1 cupful of water. Add the onion and put everything into a blender for about thirty seconds. Dissolve the vegetable paste in three cupsful of hot water. Mix in the blend and bring quickly to the boil. The *purée* need not be thickened: it can simply be served as a soup. (A *purée* can also be made from chickpeas.)

Bean Soup

½ cupful chickpea sprouts
½ cupful lentil sprouts
½ cupful boiled black-eyed beans
¼ cupful boiled brown rice
3 tablespoonsful olive oil
1 cupful chopped onion
1 litre (1¾ pt.) water
2 teaspoonsful vegetable bouillon paste

Dissolve the bouillon paste in a pot containing a little hot water. Mix in the oil, onions and chickpea sprouts. Let the mixture simmer for a few minutes. Pour in the black-eyed beans and top up with the remaining water. Bring to the boil. Add the rice and the lentil sprouts just before serving.

Soyabean Soup

2 cupsful soyabean sprouts
1 litre (1¾ pt.) water
2 finely-chopped celery sticks
½ cupful cubed carrots
1 chopped onion
1-2 teaspoonsful vegetable bouillon paste
1 teaspoonful thyme

Dissolve the bouillon paste in hot water. Add the celery, onion and carrots and boil for five minutes. Mix in ¾ cupful of soyabean sprouts with a little water in a blender and pour the mixture and the remaining soyabean sprouts into the soup. Cook over a low heat for five minutes. Thicken the soup with a little arrowroot and season with thyme or herb salt to taste.

Country Meadow Soup

$\frac{1}{2}$ cupful green pea sprouts
$\frac{1}{2}$ cupful mungbean sprouts
$2\frac{1}{2}$ cupsful water
$1\frac{1}{2}$ cupsful milk
1 carrot
1 small leek
2 tablespoonsful flour
2 tablespoonsful olive oil
1 teaspoonful vegetable bouillon paste
Parsley/wheat grass

Chop the leek and slice the carrots and *sauté* in olive oil in a saucepan over a low heat. Sprinkle on the flour, adding the water a little at a time. Add the green pea sprouts and boil for ten minutes. Add the milk, mungbean sprouts and bouillon paste. Allow the soup to boil up again. Season with herb salt, finely-chopped parsley or wheat grass.

Minestrone

½ cupful mungbean sprouts
½ cupful lentil sprouts
½ cupful chickpea sprouts
½ cupful yellow pea sprouts
1 litre (1¾ pt.) water
1 large potato
½ courgette
½ carrot
½ cupful whole wheat noodles
1 cupful olive oil
Sage
Basil
Vegetable bouillon paste
Herb salt
Grated cheese

Cut up all the vegetables into small pieces. Quickly *sauté* them in a little oil and add a little water now and again. Add the noodles and allow all the ingredients to simmer for twenty minutes. Chop the chickpea sprouts and the yellow pea sprouts and boil them over a low heat for five minutes. Sprinkle with the sage, basil and herb salt. Serve the soup hot with grated cheese.

Oriental Soup

½ cupful mungbean sprouts
½ cupful split pea sprouts
¾ cupful sliced carrots
½ cupful chopped celery
2 chopped shallots
1 litre (1¾ pt.) water
1 tablespoonful olive oil
1 teaspoonful vegetable bouillon paste
1 teaspoonful arrowroot
1 tablespoonful soysauce

Dissolve the bouillon paste and the arrowroot in hot water and add the soysauce. *Sauté* the shallots with the carrots, celery and chickpea sprouts in oil in a frying pan. Transfer this to a saucepan and cook over a low heat for twenty minutes. Add the mungbean sprouts just before serving.

Curry Soup

2 cupsful fenugreek sprouts
3 cupsful water
2 boiled potatoes
1 cupful milk
Soysauce
3 tablespoonsful olive oil
Herb salt
2-4 teaspoonsful curry powder

Dice the boiled potatoes. Boil the water and add the potatoes. *Sauté* the fenugreek sprouts in oil and add the curry powder, milk and 1 tablespoonful of soysauce. Transfer to a saucepan and bring quickly to the boil. Let the soup stand on the hot plate for five minutes before serving. You can also mix in sprouts of both three and six days growth, as they differ in taste and shape.

HOT DISHES
Sprouts in Curry Butter

1 cupful fenugreek sprouts
3 tablespoonsful butter
2-3 tablespoonsful curry powder
Dill

Melt the butter in a saucepan or frying pan. Mix in the curry powder and dill thoroughly and *sauté* together with the sprouts. Serve with rice.

You can vary this by using other sprouts and using parsley, chervil or thyme instead of the dill. This is a dish that is quick to prepare and which goes well with potatoes, rice, vegetables and vegetable rissoles.

Curry Hot Pot

1½ cupsful boiled chickpea sprouts
½ cupful fenugreek sprouts
4-5 shredded potatoes
5-7 cauliflower florets
1 small tin of green peas
1 banana
1¼ cupsful yogurt
Cashew nuts
3-6 teaspoonsful curry powder
3 tablespoonsful butter
Olive oil
Herb salt

Heat up the butter, oil and three teaspoonsful of curry powder in a saucepan. Add the potatoes, chickpea sprouts and the cauliflower florets. Add some water and stir while simmering for 15-20 minutes. Stir in the peas and the fenugreek sprouts. Take the saucepan off the heat and add the yogurt. Slice and add the banana and sprinkle with a handful of cashew nuts. Stir and heat up. Serve with a little more curry powder and herb salt to taste. Let the curry stand for a few minutes before serving it with rice.

Spaghetti With Sprout Sauce

Spaghetti
Sauce:
½ cupful lentil sprouts
½ cupful mungbean sprouts
1 onion
1-2 cloves of garlic
1½ cupsful crushed tomatoes
3 tablespoonsful tomato *purée*
1 cupful of water
1-2 teaspoonsful of arrowroot
Soysauce
Thyme
Herb salt

Chop the onion and add the mashed tomatoes, sliced garlic and sprouts and boil for 3-5 minutes in ¾ cupful of water. Dissolve the arrowroot in ¼ cupful of water mixed with the tomato puree and stir in 1-2 tablespoonsful of soybean sauce. Season with a little thyme and herb salt. Mix everything together and serve with wholemeal spaghetti and grated parmesan cheese.

Chinese Vegetables

1 cupful mungbean sprouts (using flowerpot method)
4 shallots
1 red pepper
1 green pepper
$\frac{1}{2}$ cupful mushrooms
$\frac{1}{4}$ cupful sliced leek
$\frac{3}{4}$ cupful tinned bamboo shoots
$\frac{1}{2}$ cupful olive oil
Soysauce
Arrowroot
Herb salt

Cut up all the vegetables into small pieces and *sauté* them in oil for a few minutes. Add $1\frac{1}{2}$ cupsful of water and simmer for 5-10 minutes. Dissolve 1 teaspoonful of arrowroot in a little water and stir in the vegetables. Season with soysauce and herb salt. Serve with brown rice.

Cauliflower Mountain

1 cauliflower
Mixed vegetables (e.g. maize, green peas, carrots, string beans)
Sprout sauce (see page 116)

Boil the cauliflower for ten to fifteen minutes. *Sauté* the mixed vegetables in a little oil. Put the cauliflower on a serving plate and arrange the vegetables around it. Pour the hot sprout sauce over it. Top with a sprinkling of grated cheese and finely-chopped parsley.

Sprout Ragout

- ½ cupful fenugreek sprouts
- ½ cupful mungbean sprouts
- ½ cupful lentil sprouts
- 4 soya cutlets
- 2 tomatoes
- 1 small leek
- 1 garlic clove
- 5 tablespoonsful olive oil
- 2 tablespoonsful soysauce
- 1 teaspoonful arrowroot
- 1 teaspoonful nutmeg
- Herb salt
- 2 tablespoonsful vegetable bouillon paste

Dissolve the bouillon paste in 5 cupsful of boiling water and pour it over the soya cutlets, leaving them to soak for an hour. Then put the cutlets between paper towels and squeeze out the water. Coat them with the soysauce. Shred them up and *sauté* in a little oil. Chop the leek, and the garlic and slice the tomatoes and mix them together with the sprouts. Add all these to the soya shreds and *sauté* the whole mixture for about five minutes. Dissolve the arrowroot with ½ cupful of water and pour over the mixture. Season with nutmeg and a little herb salt, and stir. Serve with brown rice.

Ratatouille

$\frac{1}{2}$ cupful aduki bean sprouts
$\frac{1}{2}$ cupful chickpea sprouts
$\frac{1}{2}$ cupful mungbean sprouts
$\frac{1}{2}$ cubed aubergine
1 sliced yellow onion
1 chopped courgette
$\frac{1}{2}$ diced cucumber
4-5 sliced tomatoes
1 shredded pepper
1 crushed garlic clove
Basil
Oregano
Herb salt
$\frac{1}{2}$ cupful olive oil

Sauté the onion, garlic and pepper in olive oil. Stir in the other vegetables and the chickpea sprouts and boil with the lid on for fifteen minutes. Remove the lid and let the mixture boil for a further ten minutes, or until it achieves the right thickness. Add the remaining sprouts. Sprinkle with finely-chopped parsley and season with basil and oregano.

Sprout Rissoles

Making sprout rissoles is a good way of using up excess sprouts. All sorts of sprouts can be used. Put the sprouts in a blender or meat mincer. The quantities of the other ingredients depend on how many sprouts you use.

Mixed sprouts
Boiled lentils
Boiled potatoes
Buckwheat flour
Breadcrumbs
Sesame seeds
Soysauce
Herb salt

Mix the flour and the mixed sprouts together. Put the potatoes with the sprout mixture through the mincer, or mix thoroughly by hand. Add the breadcrumbs and form into rissoles. Brush with soysauce and coat with ground sesame seeds. Fry gently in olive oil over a low heat.

Sprout Rissoles of Vegetable Stuffing Mix

$1\frac{1}{4}$-2 cupsful sprouts
1 packet of vegetable stuffing mix
$1\frac{1}{4}$ cupsful water
1 tablespoonful finely-chopped onion
Olive oil

Put the sprouts and the water through a blender. Mix this with the stuffing mix and the onion. Let it stand for a few minutes. Form into rissoles, cover them with ground sesame seeds and fry gently in olive oil. There are several different stuffing mixes available on the market. By adding sprouts to your rissoles you will give them a fresher flavour.

Sprout Balls

2-4 cupsful sprouts
1 small beetroot
4-5 boiled potatoes
$\frac{1}{2}$-1 cupful breadcrumbs
2 tablespoonsful olive oil
1-2 teaspoonsful kelp powder/herb salt

Cut up the potatoes and beetroot into small cubes and mix with the sprouts. Add the herb salt. Put everything through a mincer once or twice. Add some breadcrumbs if the mixture is too moist. The beetroot adds a pretty red colour. Shape into small balls and fry these gently in olive oil over a low heat. Variations of this recipe can be obtained by using different sprouts and by adding onion, garlic and soysauce as seasonings. The quantities given make about fifteen to twenty sprout balls. You can freeze those that are not eaten.

Further Information

Sprouters and sprouting seeds available from:
   Ambig Products Limited
   3 Baronsmead Road
   London SW13 9RR

   Thompson and Morgan (Ipswich) Limited
   London Road
   Ipswich
   Suffolk IP2 0BA

Sprouting seeds available from:
   G.R. Lane Health Products Limited
   Sisson Road
   Gloucester GL1 3QB

Information on sprouts and grasses available from:
   Hippocrates Health Institute
   25 Exeter Street
   Boston
   Mass. 02116
   U.S.A.

Sprouters and sprouting seeds are also available from most good health food stores.

Bibliography

Blanchard, M.P., *The Sprouter's Cookbook*, Garden Way (1975).

Cayce, E., *On Diet and Health*, Warner Books (1976).

Dinaburg, K-D'Ann Akel, *Nutritional Survival Kit: The facts and recipes you need for a safe and healthful diet*, Panjandrum Press (1977).

Hills, L.D., *Comfrey: Fodder, Food and Remedy*, University Books (1976).

Hunsberger, Mae, and Loeffler, Chris, *How I Conquered the Live Foods Gourmet*, Production House (1978).

Hunsberger, Mae, and Loeffler, Chris, *How I conquered Cancer Naturally*, A Production House Book (1975).

Jensen, B., *Health Magic Through Chlorophyll from Living Plant Life*, Microlith Printing Inc. (1977).

Kaysing, B and R., *Eat Well On a Dollar a Day*, Chronicle Books (1975).

King, M. Scott, *Food For Thought*, Castle Cary Press (1975).

Kloss, J., *The Back to Eden Cook Book*, Woodbridge Press (1974).

Kulvinskas, V., *Love your Body: Live food recipes*, OMango Press (1976).

Kulvinskas, V., *Nutritional Evaluation of Sprouts and Grasses*, OMango Press (1976).

Kulvinskas, V., *Survival into the 21st Century*, OMango Press (1976).

Lindlahr, V., *You Are What You Eat*, Newcastle (1971).

Munroe, E., *Sprouts to Grow and Eat*, The Stephen Greene Press (1974).

Oliver, M.H., *Add a Few Sprouts*, Keats (1975).

Reynolds, B.S., *How to Survive with Sprouting*, Hawkes (1973).

Stone, R., *A Purifying Diet*, (1974).

Stone, R., *Health-Building* (1974).

Tobe, J., *Sprouts, Elixir of Life*, The Provoker Press (1976).

U.S.A. Department of Agriculture, *Handbook of the Nutritional Contents of Foods*, Dover Publ (1963). Published regularly.

Weeks, D., *The Jar Garden*, Woodbridge Press (1976).

Whyte, K.C., *The Complete Sprouting Cookbook*, Troubador Press (1973).

Wigmore, A., *Be Your Own Doctor. Let Living Food Be Your Medicine*, Hippocrates Health Institute (1976).

Wigmore, A., *Why Suffer? The Answer? Wheatgrass, God's Manna!* Hippocrates Health Institute (1976).

Wigmore, A., *Spiritual-Physical Survival Through Sprouting*, Hippocrates Health Institute (1976).

Wigmore, A., *Garden Indoors, A New Concept in Diet*, Hipprocrates Health Institute (1976).

Wigmore, A., *Indoor Organic Gardening for Health*, The Today Church, Texas.

Wilson, F., *Successful Sprouting*, Thorsons Ltd. (1978).

Index

aduki beans, 30, 56, 82, 106, 119
alfalfa, 8, 25, 30, 32, 33, 48, 49, 51, 57, 75, 78, 81, 82, 83, 86, 87, 91, 93, 94, 95, 98, 99, 106
Alfalfa Loaf, 93
amino acids, 13, 56, 64
Autumn Plate, 78
Avocado Dressing, 84
Avocado with Cottage Cheese, 98

Bailey, Dr C.W., 16
Bean Grotto, 79
Bean Soup, 110
Big Mac Special, 94
buckwheat, 30, 32, 65
Budget Salad, 80
Burkholder, Paul, 15

Calzone, 106
Cannelloni, 102
carbohydrates, 13
carotene, 15, 57, 68
Cauliflower Gratin, 108
Cauliflower Salad, 82
Celeriac Gratin, 107
Cheese Salad, 83
chickpeas, 30, 31, 33, 48, 78, 80, 81, 97, 99, 110, 112, 115, 119
Chinese Vegetables, 117
chlorophyll, 15, 20, 31, 38, 57, 67, 71
Cook, Captain, 7

Country Meadow Soup, 111
Courgettes with Sprouts, 100
cress, 40, 44, 48, 65, 75
Curry Hot Pot, 115
Curry Soup, 113

dandelion leaves, 80
Dolmades, 101

Earp-Thomas, Dr, 20
Everyday Salad, 80

fennel, 30, 81, 83
fenugreek, 25, 30, 58, 75, 80, 82, 83, 86, 91, 99, 101, 105, 106, 107, 113, 114, 118
Fetta Cheese Salad, 83
Filled Pancakes, 103
Fischer, Dr Hans, 20
food additives, 8

garbanzo beans, see chickpeas
Green Pea Purée, 109
green pea sprouts, 111

Hagiwara, Dr Y., 23
Herb Dressing, 85
Hippocrates, 19
Honey Dressing, 85
Hunsberger, Eydie Mae, 22

Knowles, John H., 19

Kulvinskas, Viktoras, 22

lecithin, 62
lentils, 25, 30, 51, 60, 78, 81, 87, 91, 99, 100, 101, 105, 106, 107, 108, 110, 112, 116, 118

Mashed Potato Grotto, 79
millet, 65
Minestrone, 112
Mini Burger, 94
Mini Pizza, 92
mungbeans, 25, 33, 51, 56, 61, 78, 80, 83, 91, 94, 95, 99, 106, 108, 111, 112, 113, 116, 117, 118, 119
mustard seeds, 40, 44, 65, 95

nettle sprouts, 80

Oriental Soup, 113

Party Loaf, 91
peas, 64
Pizza fillings, 105
Pizza Salad, 83
polyunsaturated fats, 13
Potato Burger, 95
Potato Salad, 82
Protein Salad, 81
proteins, 13, 58, 59, 60, 61, 62, 63, 64

Quattro Stagione Pizza, 106

radish seeds, 30, 44, 65
Ratatouille, 119
Red Cabbage Salad, 82
red soyabean, *see* aduki beans
rice, 65
Rice Grotto, 79
Royal Yacht Britannia, 87

Sahlin, Sigri, 23
saturated fats, 13
Sesame Dressing, 84
sesame seeds, 65, 84
Ship Ahoy Sandwich, 87
Simple Pizza Dough, 104

soyabeans, 28, 31, 33, 48, 59, 62, 81, 110
Soyabean Soup, 110
Spaghetti with Sprout Sauce, 116
Spring Plate, 78
Sprout Balls, 121
Sprout Burger, 95
Sprout Canoe, 98
Sprout Pocket, 97
Sprout Ragout, 118
Sprout Rissole, 120
Sprout Sandwich with Mushroom, 91
Sprout Tube, 97
sprouts
  healing properties of, 19-23
  nutritional value of, 13-18
  storage of, 29
Sprouts in Curry Butter, 114
spruce shoots, 80
Stuffed Peppers, 99
Stuffed Tomatoes, 99
Summer Plate, 77
Sunflower Dressing, 84
sunflower seeds, 28, 30, 68, 84
sunflower shoots, 80, 95
Sweetcorn Salad, 81
Sweetheart Sandwich, 86

Triplet Salad, 81

Vitamin Sandwich, 86
vitamins
  A, 58, 59, 60, 61, 64
  B-complex, 13, 15, 16, 31, 60, 62, 63, 64
  C, 10, 13, 15, 16, 59, 60, 61, 62, 63, 64, 68
  E, 13, 60, 61, 63, 68

wheat, 63, 75
wheatgrass, 20, 25, 26, 28, 67-71
wheatgrass juice, 21, 26, 71
Wigmore, Ann, 7, 20, 21-2, 25, 67, 68, 70
Winter Plate, 78

Yellow Pea Soup, 109

Index

aduki beans, 30, 56, 82, 106, 119
alfalfa, 8, 25, 30, 32, 33, 48, 49, 51, 57, 75, 78, 81, 82, 83, 86, 87, 91, 93, 94, 95, 98, 99, 106
Alfalfa Loaf, 93
amino acids, 13, 56, 64
Autumn Plate, 78
Avocado Dressing, 84
Avocado with Cottage Cheese, 98

Bailey, Dr C.W., 16
Bean Grotto, 79
Bean Soup, 110
Big Mac Special, 94
buckwheat, 30, 32, 65
Budget Salad, 80
Burkholder, Paul, 15

Calzone, 106
Cannelloni, 102
carbohydrates, 13
carotene, 15, 57, 68
Cauliflower Gratin, 108
Cauliflower Salad, 82
Celeriac Gratin, 107
Cheese Salad, 83
chickpeas, 30, 31, 33, 48, 78, 80, 81, 97, 99, 110, 112, 115, 119
Chinese Vegetables, 117
chlorophyll, 15, 20, 31, 38, 57, 67, 71
Cook, Captain, 7

Country Meadow Soup, 111
Courgettes with Sprouts, 100
cress, 40, 44, 48, 65, 75
Curry Hot Pot, 115
Curry Soup, 113

dandelion leaves, 80
Dolmades, 101

Earp-Thomas, Dr, 20
Everyday Salad, 80

fennel, 30, 81, 83
fenugreek, 25, 30, 58, 75, 80, 82, 83, 86, 91, 99, 101, 105, 106, 107, 113, 114, 118
Fetta Cheese Salad, 83
Filled Pancakes, 103
Fischer, Dr Hans, 20
food additives, 8

garbanzo beans, see chickpeas
Green Pea Purée, 109
green pea sprouts, 111

Hagiwara, Dr Y., 23
Herb Dressing, 85
Hippocrates, 19
Honey Dressing, 85
Hunsberger, Eydie Mae, 22

Knowles, John H., 19

Kulvinskas, Viktoras, 22

lecithin, 62
lentils, 25, 30, 51, 60, 78, 81, 87, 91, 99, 100, 101, 105, 106, 107, 108, 110, 112, 116, 118

Mashed Potato Grotto, 79
millet, 65
Minestrone, 112
Mini Burger, 94
Mini Pizza, 92
mungbeans, 25, 33, 51, 56, 61, 78, 80, 83, 91, 94, 95, 99, 106, 108, 111, 112, 113, 116, 117, 118, 119
mustard seeds, 40, 44, 65, 95

nettle sprouts, 80

Oriental Soup, 113

Party Loaf, 91
peas, 64
Pizza fillings, 105
Pizza Salad, 83
polyunsaturated fats, 13
Potato Burger, 95
Potato Salad, 82
Protein Salad, 81
proteins, 13, 58, 59, 60, 61, 62, 63, 64

Quattro Stagione Pizza, 106

radish seeds, 30, 44, 65
Ratatouille, 119
Red Cabbage Salad, 82
red soyabean, see aduki beans
rice, 65
Rice Grotto, 79
Royal Yacht Britannia, 87

Sahlin, Sigri, 23
saturated fats, 13
Sesame Dressing, 84
sesame seeds, 65, 84
Ship Ahoy Sandwich, 87
Simple Pizza Dough, 104

soyabeans, 28, 31, 33, 48, 59, 62, 81, 110
Soyabean Soup, 110
Spaghetti with Sprout Sauce, 116
Spring Plate, 78
Sprout Balls, 121
Sprout Burger, 95
Sprout Canoe, 98
Sprout Pocket, 97
Sprout Ragout, 118
Sprout Rissole, 120
Sprout Sandwich with Mushroom, 91
Sprout Tube, 97
sprouts
  healing properties of, 19-23
  nutritional value of, 13-18
  storage of, 29
Sprouts in Curry Butter, 114
spruce shoots, 80
Stuffed Peppers, 99
Stuffed Tomatoes, 99
Summer Plate, 77
Sunflower Dressing, 84
sunflower seeds, 28, 30, 68, 84
sunflower shoots, 80, 95
Sweetcorn Salad, 81
Sweetheart Sandwich, 86

Triplet Salad, 81

Vitamin Sandwich, 86
vitamins
  A, 58, 59, 60, 61, 64
  B-complex, 13, 15, 16, 31, 60, 62, 63, 64
  C, 10, 13, 15, 16, 59, 60, 61, 62, 63, 64, 68
  E, 13, 60, 61, 63, 68

wheat, 63, 75
wheatgrass, 20, 25, 26, 28, 67-71
wheatgrass juice, 21, 26, 71
Wigmore, Ann, 7, 20, 21-2, 25, 67, 68, 70
Winter Plate, 78

Yellow Pea Soup, 109